Bug-Free
Organic Gardening

Bug-Free
Organic Gardening

Controlling Pest Insects without Chemicals

Anna Hess

Skyhorse Publishing

Skyhorse Publishing books may be purchased in bulk at special discounts for sales promotion, corporate gifts, fund-raising, or educational purposes. Special editions can also be created to specifications. For details, contact the Special Sales Department, Skyhorse Publishing, 307 West 36th Street, 11th Floor, New York, NY 10018 or info@skyhorsepublishing.com.

Skyhorse® and Skyhorse Publishing® are registered trademarks of Skyhorse Publishing, Inc.®, a Delaware corporation.

Visit our website at www.skyhorsepublishing.com.

10 9 8 7 6 5 4 3

Library of Congress Cataloging-in-Publication Data is available on file.

Cover design by Qualcom

Print ISBN: 978-1-5107-4198-0
Ebook ISBN: 978-1-5107-4202-4

Printed in China

Contents

Introduction

Many leaf nibblers, like this bush katydid (*Scudderia* sp.), are solitary and go largely unnoticed in the garden.

Insects are one of the worst problems facing many organic fruit and vegetable growers, and I was certainly no exception at the beginning of my homesteading career. For the last twelve years, my husband and I have grown most of our own food, and some days I was ready to throw in the towel. Our squash plants melted into puddles of wilted leaves just before they set fruit (vine borers at work), tiny grubs defoliated our asparagus fronds (asparagus beetles chowing down), and mysterious insects arrived in the night to eat our Swiss chard leaves (striped blister beetles being bad). Our broccoli was so covered in cabbageworms that it seemed easier to toss the food than to eat it, and Japanese beetles dripped from our grapevines.

Our neighbors told us to spray, but even seemingly safe pesticides like Bt and neem oil gave me the willies. Wasn't there a way to grow our food without any chemical inputs at all?

The answer was yes, but only once we learned to bend a little to nature's whims. A garden ecosystem is always going to be at least slightly out of balance because humans have manipulated the soil and landscape to promote productivity, but we can still do our best to bring natural forces to bear against insect pests. My husband and I beat squash vine borers with variety selection and succession planting, we waited for natural predators to defeat the asparagus and blister beetles, we learned to plant our broccoli at a time when cabbage moths were dormant, and we switched over to a variety of grape that Japanese beetles don't enjoy. With these and other techniques, we eventually learned to keep pest insects in check without spraying anything at all. Using the tips in this book, you can do the same in your own garden!

(As a final side note before you delve into the meat of natural insect control, I wanted to alert you to the presence of a glossary in the back of this book. Now and then I'll use a term like "permaculture" or "Bt" and will assume you know what I'm talking about. If you do—great! If not, just flip to the glossary for a quick refresher course on these advanced homesteading topics.)

What Is a Naturally Bug-Free Garden?

A praying mantis moved into a bed of buggy beans in search of a high-protein snack.

Is a naturally bug-free garden a spot where no creepy crawlies of any sort reside? Far from it! In fact, if you follow my lead and use the bug-control methods outlined in this book, you'll soon see bees on your squash flowers and mantises in your beans. Beneficials will be everywhere.

And your garden won't even really be free of pest invertebrates. It's necessary to keep the bad guys around in low numbers in order to attract the good guys, so you'll still see the occasional slug and cucumber beetle. On the other hand, you'll no longer find plants so overcome by the bad bugs that they can't hold their heads up high, so you might stop noticing the pests entirely as nature takes over the job of keeping bad-bug populations in check.

When it comes right down to it, the only thing a naturally bug-free garden is really free of is the gardener's need to wage war against pests. It's the *gardener*, not the garden, who is set free. And that freedom is what we were really looking for all along, isn't it?

PART 1

The Garden Ecosystem

The presence of centipedes and other predators is a sign your garden is in balance.

Chapter 1:
Identifying Your Bugs

I was concerned when I first noticed these dark scales on dead asparagus stalks, but I soon realized they were simply the eggs of the innocuous katydid that sings me to sleep on autumn nights.

Many new gardeners assume that every bug is a bad bug, but the truth is that a significant number of the creepy crawlies you'll find on your vegetables are either random passers-by, are beneficial pollinators, or are predators of leaf nibblers. The trick is to know the difference, and to understand how larger animals fit into the complex web of garden life.

Since it's so easy to mistake good bugs for bad bugs, my first rule when dealing with garden insects is to identify everything I see. *Bug-Free Organic Gardening* is too short to introduce every garden character, but this chapter will at least give you a frame of reference to fit unidentified bugs into, along with an idea of key identification resources. Between the identification tips found here and the profiles in later chapters of common garden friends and foes, you should soon be able to name most critters that show up in your yard.

Types of Invertebrates

Common Garden Invertebrates

Arthropods

Annelids
earthworms

Mollusks
snails, slugs

Myriapods
centipedes,
millipedes

Arachnids
spiders,
mites

Crustaceans
woodlice
(aka sowbugs)

Insects

Beetles

Flies

True Bugs

Grasshoppers

Dragonflies

Butterflies/Moths

Mantids

Ants/Bees/Wasps

The most common types of invertebrates visible to the naked eye in a garden are annelids (worms), mollusks (snails and slugs), myriapods (centipedes and millipedes), arachnids (spiders and mites), crustaceans (woodlice and crayfish), and insects.

Your first step when you find an unknown bug should be to figure out which large categories the animal fits into. Starting at the top, nearly all garden bugs are known as invertebrates because they have no backbone. (I incorrectly call them "bugs" throughout this book when I'm not feeling very scientific.)

The chart opposite shows the wide range of invertebrates you can find in most backyards. The major categories include annelids (worms), mollusks (snails and slugs), myriapods (centipedes and millipedes), arachnids (spiders and mites), crustaceans (woodlice and crayfish), and insects. Among insects, the most common categories are beetles (with hard wing covers), flies (with only one pair of flight wings, the other wing pair having been reduced to knobs), true bugs (with sucking mouthparts and including cicadas, aphids, leafhoppers, and shield bugs), grasshoppers and their kin (including crickets and katydids), butterflies and moths (and the caterpillars that are their larvae), hymenoptera (ants, bees, and wasps), and dragonflies (along with the related damselflies). If you can tell these major groups of insects apart, you'll be well on your way to identifying the next unknown bug in your garden.

Identification Resources

It's handy to be familiar with each stage of an insect's life cycle. The photos here all show Mexican bean beetles: eggs, a larva, and an adult.

When I find an unknown denizen of the garden, I usually start my identification campaign with the Internet. If you go to www .images.google.com and type in some identifying features, your pest's mugshot may pop right up. For example, when I saw my first asparagus beetles, I typed in "orange beetle on asparagus," and the species I was looking for turned up on the first row. You'll notice that a good search often includes the category of invertebrate, its color, and the plant the bug is found on.

If a simple image search fails, I turn to books next. *Garden Insects of North America* by Whitney Cranshaw is my favorite invertebrate field guide because its full-color photos usually help me narrow down my search quickly. Several other field guides to garden insects (or just to insects in general) also exist, and any of these titles can help you identify your garden friends and foes.

But sometimes books fail me. At that point, I usually turn to www.bugguide.net, which is the Wikipedia of the invertebrate

Earthworms are one of the classic beneficial invertebrates.

world. I can often identify an invertebrate (or at least get close) by working my way through BugGuide's key, but if I'm thoroughly stumped, I instead log in and submit a photo, requesting identification help. One of the volunteers gets back to me within a day or two, telling me which species (or category) of invertebrate I've found. Those of you less technologically inclined may get the same results by capturing the questionable insect in a jar and taking it to your local agricultural extension agent for identification. (Simply search "agricultural extension office" at maps. google.com to find the closest extension agent to you.)

No matter which method of identification you end up using, I urge you not to skip this step! I focused on insect identification first for a reason—you can't work to promote the good bugs and minimize the bad bugs if you can't tell them apart.

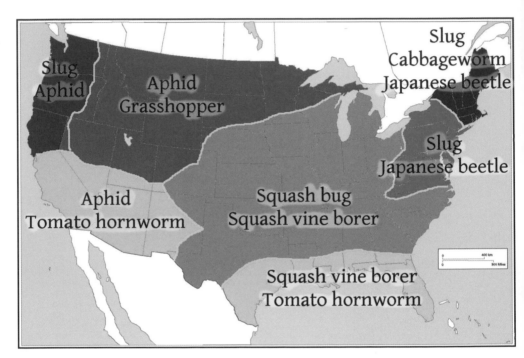

A survey by *Mother Earth News* showed that home gardeners' worst pests varied by location.

Chapter 2: Worst Garden Pests

Although you probably won't be able to identify every single invertebrate in your garden anytime soon, it's worth knowing the worst offenders on sight. To that end, this chapter includes a brief rundown of the natural history and common treatment methods used for the twelve worst pests in home gardens (based on a *Mother Earth News* survey of 1,300 gardeners). As you read, please keep in mind that many of the mainstream organic treatments mentioned in this chapter aren't quite as kind to the earth as a permaculture gardener might like. I'll suggest alternatives later in the text, and you can also check the glossary for more information about the potential dangers of chemicals mentioned here.

Aphids

Aphids are often found in large colonies being tended by ants. The aphids benefit from predator protection, while the ants are allowed to consume excess plant sap that shoots through the aphids' system before it can be digested.

Aphids include many species of tiny insects that suck the juices out of plants. I find it interesting that aphids rank #3 on *Mother Earth News*'s survey of worst garden pests because, in my own garden, the tiny critters only show up when I'm guilty of over-fertilization. Even then, aphids are quickly wiped out by natural predators.

Mother Earth News gardeners treat aphids by pruning off infected plant parts, by attracting beneficial insects, and by applying insecticidal soap. I recommend first lowering the nitrogen content of your fertilization campaign, then ensuring that you have plenty of natural predators to go around.

Who are these natural predators that do such a good job of controlling aphids? Ladybugs are the best-known of the common aphid eaters, but tiny wasps will also show up to parasitize the problematic juice suckers. Meanwhile, lacewing larvae, minute pirate bugs, hoverfly larvae, big-eyed bugs, damsel bugs, and the larvae of predatory midges feed on aphids as well. Letting aphid populations thrive unchecked will attract many of these predators, the flowers I list in chapter 11 will boost the populations of other predators, and a shallow water source like a bird bath full of stones will bring predatory midges to your yard.

Cabbageworms

The most common species of cabbageworm is the larva of the cabbage white (*Pieris rapae*), sometimes confusingly called a "cabbage moth" even though it is really a type of butterfly.

The southern cabbageworm is the larva of the related checkered white (*Pontia protodice*), which is found primarily in the southern United States. A few other caterpillars are also sometimes called cabbageworms.

Cabbageworms come in multiple species, but most of you will only run across the two most common types mentioned here. The green caterpillar of the cabbage white is the most widespread nibbler on crucifer leaves, and I find this cabbageworm easy to control by hand-picking in my own garden. Southern cabbageworms are much harder to manage since the spotted caterpillars tend to live inside the florets of broccoli plants, where the caterpillars are inaccessible until after harvest. (See chapter 10 for tips on debugging problematic harvests in the kitchen.)

Mother Earth News gardeners have reported luck with control strategies that include Bt, spinosad, row covers, and promoting caterpillar predators (such as paper wasps and yellow jackets). Timing seems to be relatively effective in my garden, since the cabbageworms are killed (or at least slowed down) by frosts in the late fall and early spring. If we can get our broccoli and cabbage sets out into the garden early enough in the spring, we see little damage before harvest; similarly, a late-fall planting also misses the peak cabbageworm season. With cabbageworm populations minimized due to careful crop timing, I'm able to round out my control campaign with variety selection (chapter 5) and hand-picking (chapter 7).

Corn Earworms

Photo credit: Ruth Hazzard, University of Massachusetts.

Corn earworms are largely a cosmetic problem in the home garden.

Corn earworms (*Helicoverpa zea*) are caterpillars that tunnel into ears of corn, as well as into tomatoes and a few other crops. Despite being on the *Mother Earth News* top-pest list, I consider earworms to be only a cosmetic problem in our garden. Most of our ears of corn never get damaged, and it's easy to break off the affected portion on those that do. If you can't stand blemished fruit, though, you can prevent earworm damage by applying vegetable oil or Bt to the tips of ears when silks start to show, or by planting varieties with tight ear tips. (See chapter 5 for more information on resistant vegetable varieties.)

Cucumber Beetles

Cucumber beetles include two species: striped cucumber beetles (*Acalymma vittata*) and spotted cucumber beetles (*Diabrotica undecimpunctata howardi*). Both feed on melon and cucumber plants, transferring a bacterial disease known as "wilt" to the vegetables. Bacterial wilt symptoms begin with drooping of the leaves, followed by death of the plant. For a definitive diagnosis, cut the cucurbit's stem and squeeze the cut ends—if the plant has succumbed to bacterial wilt, a sticky sap will ooze out and will form a long thread when you touch the two cut ends back together then slowly pull them apart again.

Cucumber beetles are problematic because they carry bacterial wilt disease.

Mother Earth News gardeners recommend hand-picking cucumber beetles, treating with neem oil, cleaning up the garden to prevent overwintering locations, and utilizing poultry, row covers, companion planting, and yellow sticky traps. I simply succession plant my cucumbers (chapter 4), don't plant the ultra-susceptible cantaloupes, choose resistant varieties of both cucumbers and watermelons (chapter 5), and try trap crops (chapter 8).

Cutworms

Cutworms are caterpillars that live in the soil and feed on young plants. Their pupae are often found in the soil in the spring.

Cutworms are often invisible in the garden since they live in the soil, but you'll know you have these pesky caterpillars if your seedlings are beheaded in the night. Cutworms belong to any of several species of moths, but the most common type in North American gardens is the variegated cutworm (*Peridroma saucia*). *Mother Earth News* gardeners recommend making little collars around the bases of seedlings to protect them from damage, cultivating soil before planting, or setting out larger seedings (a good choice with cutworm favorites like broccoli). Natural predators seem to keep cutworms under control in our garden

Herrick Kimball, author of *The Planet Whizbang Idea Book for Gardeners*, uses split goldenrod stems to protect seedlings from cutworms.

Photo credit: Herrick Kimball, www.whizbangbooks.blogspot.com.

during most years, and I always germinate enough seedlings that I can replace any transplants that get eaten in the night.

Grasshoppers

Grasshoppers include a number of species that eat leaves but that are rarely a problem in the vegetable garden. Most pest grasshoppers are members of the genus *Melanoplus*, including two-striped grasshoppers (*M. bivittatus*), differential grasshoppers (*M. differentialis*), migratory grasshoppers (*M. sanguinipes*), and redlegged grasshoppers (*M. femurrubrum*). Besides eating grass, grasshoppers enjoy the leaves of beans, leafy greens, and corn. *Mother Earth News* gardeners treat grasshopper infestations with hungry chickens and guinea fowl while I rely on natural garden predators to keep grasshopper populations under control.

A grasshopper sheds its tough skin like a snake does, allowing the insect to grow larger.

Japanese Beetles

Japanese beetles (*Popillia japonica*) are iridescent insects that come out of the ground for a couple of months in the summer, during which time they can completely defoliate their favorite plants (especially roses, grapes, and cherries). During the rest of the year, Japanese beetles live as white grubs

Japanese beetles often congregate in clusters as males compete to mate with a female.

in the soil, where the larval beetles do some damage feeding on plant roots.

My primary method of controlling these invasive beetles is hand-picking the adult insects (chapter 7), along with choosing plant species and varieties that are a less attractive source of food (which I'll explain in more depth in chapter 5). *Mother Earth News* gardeners add the use of trap crops, chickens, guinea fowl, ducks, robins, and bluebirds. In particular, they recommend letting birds work over the ground in late spring when beetle larvae are close to the surface and can be easily scratched up.

One seemingly innovative approach to Japanese-beetle control is to use purchased pheromones to attract Japanese beetles to sticky traps in the spring. Some gardeners even go so far as to put the lures above a funnel that feeds into a PVC pipe and drops the crunchy treats into a cup of water at chicken eye level. Unfortunately, the home gardener should be aware that studies of the efficacy of these traps show that the pheromone not only attracts the beetles that come out of your soil . . . the scent also brings in all of your neighbors' bugs as well. Since many of the attracted Japanese beetles settle onto plants around the trap rather than being captured by the sticky paper or chicken funnel, gardeners who use Japanese-beetle lures usually see higher, rather than lower, populations of these troublesome insects in their yards. I guess the lures aren't such a good idea for the home gardener after all.

Slugs

Slugs (and their shelled relatives, snails) tend to top the list of problematic pests in areas that stay cool and damp during the summer, especially among gardeners who use heavy mulches. However, you shouldn't jump to the conclusion that any mollusk you find in the garden is bad news. Unlike many of the pests mentioned in this chapter, the term "slug" is a very general one,

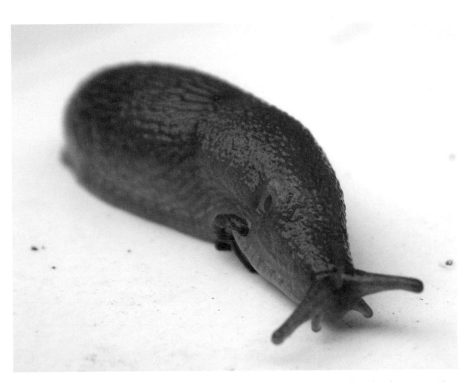

Slugs thrive in damp climates and tend to multiply in gardens topped with a heavy coating of mulch.

and saying "slugs are bad for gardens" is a lot like saying "birds are bad for gardens." While it's true that many slugs chew on leaves, others are decomposers that break down the dead plant matter on the soil surface (like your straw mulch), while a few even eat other slugs.

How can you tell the difference between good slugs and bad slugs? I generally consider any invertebrate in the garden good until I'm proven wrong, which in a slug's case consists of catching the mollusk in the act of eating my lettuce or strawberries. If you want to learn slug identification, the worst slugs include the milky garden slug (*Deroceras reticulatum*), midget milky garden slug (*Deroceras agreste*), marsh slug (*Deroceras laeve*), great gray garden slug (*Limax maximus*), and tawny garden slug (*Limax flavus*). Those of you living in the Pacific Northwest will be relieved to hear that the banana slug (*Ariolimax* spp.) is not a garden pest.

Mother Earth News readers report good luck with slug-control methods including hand-picking, iron-phosphate baits, diatomaceous earth, beer traps, chickens, garter snakes, and ducks. (More on ducks in chapter 12—the poultry aren't always as well-behaved in the garden as some books suggest.) My recommendation? Don't till. Cultivating soil tends to kill natural predators of slugs (like toads, salamanders, and snakes), and if you devastate the predator population, mulching will soon result in a garden overrun with slimy nibblers. However, if you don't churn up your soil, mollusks' natural enemies provide quite adequate slug control.

For over a decade, I lived in an area that averages a full inch of rain per week, much of my garden was located in partial shade, and our groundwater was very high. Suffice it to say that our garden stayed pretty soppy. But slugs were only a minor problem amid our vegetables because we worked hard to promote predator populations and we never tilled the ground. My conclusion is that, if you live in a slug-friendly part of the country, you should either till and don't mulch or (better) mulch and don't till.

Photo credit: Ria Malloy, University of Maryland Extension.

Squash Bugs

Squash bugs (*Anasa tristis*) suck the juices out of the leaves of cucurbits (especially pumpkins and squash), causing them to wilt. Hand-picking is a

Squash bug adults look a bit like stink bugs. Their eggs are found in V-shaped clusters between plant veins, where the eggs hatch into greenish larvae that later turn pale gray.

particularly effective method of squash-bug control, especially if you catch the insects at the egg stage. In addition, boards on the ground beside your squash plants provide a nighttime hiding place for adult squash bugs, which are easy to crush the next morning.

Mother Earth News readers also recommend cleaning up infested plants, applying neem oil to egg clusters and juvenile bugs, protecting plants with row covers, and utilizing late planting. In my own garden, I plant resistant varieties (see chapter 5), especially butternuts. Finally, one of my readers recommends using ragweed to attract praying mantises that in turn eat the problematic squash bugs. See chapter 11 for more on the ragweed version of squash-bug control.

Squash Vine Borers

Squash vine borers can be hard to see, but an infestation is evident when squash plants collapse overnight.

Squash vine borers (*Melittia cucurbitae*) are often identified by their symptoms rather than by seeing the insects themselves.

A happy squash plant will suddenly wilt and then perish even though water is abundant, proving that vine borers have eaten their way through the stem. I'll discuss my methods for controlling this pesky insect in chapters 4 and 5, so here I'll just list *Mother Earth News* gardeners' treatments: crop rotation, resistant varieties, mounding dirt over stems to promote rooting at nodes, and late planting.

Tomato and Tobacco Hornworms

Tomato hornworms (*Manduca quinquemaculata*) and tobacco hornworms (*Manduca sexta*) are large, green caterpillars that eat the leaves of tomato plants before transforming into hummingbird-like sphinx moths. As you can see from the white sacs in the photo, our hornworm problem is always controlled quickly by braconid wasps, which lay their eggs just under the skin of the caterpillar.

White cocoons on this hornworm are a sign that the caterpillar has been eaten alive from the inside out by parasitoid wasps.

The baby wasps feed on the body of the hornworm, then the parasitoids push their way to the outside of their host to spin cocoons. After transforming into adults within their cocoons, the wasps chew their way free so they can mate and lay eggs on more caterpillars. If you see hornworms similarly parasitized, leave them alone and the tiny wasps will soon spread throughout your garden.

Along with encouraging braconid wasps, *Mother Earth News* gardeners use hand-picking and Bt to control tomato and tobacco hornworms. In addition, a recent study suggests that tomato plants are able to respond to the chewing action of hornworms by creating compounds in their leaves that will kill up to a third of future munchers—see chapter 3 for more information on this type of plant defense. In other words, it's quite possible that even if you see hornworms in your garden, the pests are nothing to worry about since the garden ecosystem already has the problem well in hand.

Whiteflies

Whiteflies (*Trialeurodes vaporariorum* and related species) are tiny, winged insects that suck the juices out of plants, much like aphids do. Like aphids, I never have problems with whiteflies unless I've blocked out their natural predators, such as when I grow fall

Whiteflies are usually found on houseplants and in greenhouses.

greens under quick hoops or when I take houseplants inside over the winter. *Mother Earth News* gardeners treat whiteflies with insecticidal soaps, but I generally just wait until I'm able to put the houseplants outside, allowing natural predators to demolish pest populations. Since whiteflies can't withstand freezing temperatures, you can also uncover moderately hardy garden plants during light freezes to devastate whitefly infestations.

Other Bad Bugs

In addition to this dirty dozen of problematic insects, runners-up include: Mexican bean beetles (*Epilachna varivestis*, discussed in chapter 5), Colorado potato beetles (*Leptinotarsa decemlineata*), flea beetles (several species in subfamily Alticinae, discussed in chapter 6), and asparagus beetles (*Crioceris asparagi*, discussed in chapter 3).

And then there are the insects that many gardeners consider pests, but that don't actually prey on your plants. For example, yellow jackets may sting you, but these wasps are actually beneficial insects in the garden since they eat large quantities of caterpillars and other bad bugs. I'm not going to cover "pests" that are only bad because they bother humans, but I will touch on other problematic insects later in this book.

In addition, you'll also want to keep your eyes open and to watch what chews on your leaves and what visits your flowers since each garden has its own unique array of problematic insects and beneficials. Your yard may be home to a species I didn't think to mention here, but chances are good that one of the control techniques I suggest will wipe out your bad bugs as well as it does mine.

PART

Controlling Pests

Japanese beetles are one of the insects I control by hand-picking.

Digger wasps are supposed to prey on Japanese beetles, but we see few digger wasps and lots of beetles in my garden.

Chapter 3:
Letting Nature Take
Its Course

Now that you've been introduced to the cast of characters, it's time to look deeper into the techniques involved in keeping pests at bay. But I want to start with a much less hands-on method than trap cropping or organic pesticides. In fact, my own first line of defense when a bad bug shows up in my garden generally consists of waiting and hoping.

The theory underlying this strategy is that nearly every pest insect has several predators ready and willing to eat the bad guy up. But the predators don't have any reason to head to your yard

Asparagus beetles defoliated my asparagus plantings during our first couple of gardening years.

until the pest insects reach a certain level—who wants to comb through an entire orchard in search of one colony of aphids? As a result, you sometimes have to hold onto your temper and let pest insect populations reach critical mass in hopes of attracting their predators.

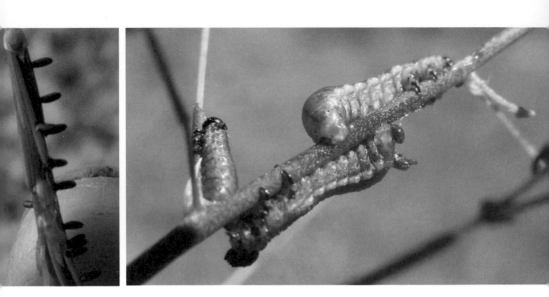

I didn't know what I was seeing when the first asparagus beetle eggs and larvae showed up on my plants.

My experience with asparagus beetles taught me the importance of this often-overlooked pest-insect remedy. I used to think of asparagus as a do-nothing vegetable, so I wasn't terribly concerned when I first saw tiny grubs nibbling on my asparagus leaves. But within a couple of weeks, entire plants were defoliated!

Research suggested my garden was suffering from an infestation of asparagus beetles, which lay their eggs in lines along asparagus fronds, with the eggs then hatching into voracious caterpillar-like grubs. Asparagus beetles can go through several generations per year, so if you don't do anything and the beetles have no predators, large plantings of asparagus can be killed back to the ground. That means you won't be eating many spears next spring.

Traditional asparagus-beetle control consists of spraying Bt, but I'm leery of that method since Bt is a relatively broad-spectrum insecticide (even if it is based on a bacterium). So, during the first year of our infestation, I hand-picked. (More on hand-picking in chapter 7.) This was a particularly difficult project since asparagus fronds are tender and you really have to squish beetle eggs to kill them, plus it's hard to find the grubs and eggs amid all that greenery. To cut a long story short, the beetles won round one.

However, the next year I knew what I was looking for and I instituted early-and-often hand-picking. That fall, I cut down all of the dead fronds and raked up the mulch, adding the debris to the chicken coop for our flock to pick over. It also helped that I started squishing the asparagus beetles immediately upon their arrival that year, so my harvests broke the earliest cycles of asparagus beetles' egg-laying.

But the tides didn't really turn until predatory stink bugs moved in. During the height of the asparagus-beetle infestation, I noticed the first of these beneficial insects dining, but one bug wasn't able to make much of a dent in the beetle population. However, by the next year, there were enough stink bugs and few enough beetles that the former were able to keep the latter in check. Recently, my only nod toward asparagus-beetle control has been to squash one or two adult beetles and perhaps ten eggs in the spring, then to step back and let the predatory stink bugs do the rest of the work.

Which brings me back to the moral of the story. If I had sprayed Bt when the infestation began, the asparagus-beetle population wouldn't have built up to the point where predatory stink bugs came

A predatory stink bug has impaled an asparagus-beetle grub on its long snout.

to call. And the chemical could also have harmed the nearby beneficial insects, so it's possible that there wouldn't have been any predatory stink bugs around to hunt down the beetles that survived. This is the primary reason I eschew chemicals (even organic ones) in the garden. Sometimes, doing nothing will yield much better long-term results . . . as long as you can hold onto your temper in the meantime.

Natural Plant Defenses

Slightly holey plants still produce copious Brussels sprouts, which may be tastier and more nutritious due to the insect damage.

Imagine a caterpillar hatching out of its egg and beginning to munch on a Brussels sprout leaf. Most gardeners think that the Brussels sprout is defenseless unless a human helper comes along to squash that marauder. The plant knows better. As soon as juices in the caterpillar's mouth interact with the open wound on the plant leaf, the Brussels sprout realizes that there are herbivores in the area. Immediately, the plant releases a chemical into the air that attracts parasitoid wasps. The wasps home in on the plant-produced scent then lay their eggs in the caterpillar's body, eating the caterpillar alive from the inside out.

Scientists are just beginning to understand the vast array of natural defenses that plants use to fend off insects when gardeners aren't around to step in. Only a few instances of plants attracting predatory insects are known so far, but many vegetables create herbivore-unfriendly chemicals in their leaves as soon as a caterpillar, aphid, or other insect begins to chow down. The chemicals are costly for the plants to produce, slowing down both growth and fruit ripening, but the compounds are worth it since they kill or damage the nibbling insects and let the wounded plant bounce back.

Plants are also willing to alert their neighbors about insect problems, with the result that an entire planting block can become resistant after an herbivore has nibbled on a single leaf. Plants communicate by emitting chemicals into the air, passing cues through roots and mycorrhizal connections, and possibly even by making sounds. In all of these cases, the neighboring plants respond by beefing up their own defenses so that herbivores will have to look elsewhere for a snack.

What does all of this mean for the gardener? First of all, low levels of bad insects should probably be left alone since their presence will help plants protect themselves from other herbivores in the neighborhood. But you might also be interested to learn that many of the chemicals that fruits and vegetables use to keep away herbivores are the same chemicals that make for a healthy human diet. For example, cabbages build antioxidants into their leaves to keep away pests, and those same antioxidants help prevent cancer in people who eat affected cabbage leaves. I wouldn't be surprised if the deeply delicious flavors of organic vegetables are also the result of compounds created by plants for the purpose of keeping bugs at bay. Yet another reason to let nature take its course . . . within reason.

Chapter 4:
Timing Plantings to
Bypass Bugs

The ecosystem-level approach to insect control that I explained in the last chapter is the best long-term solution to bug problems in the garden. But the technique can feel painfully slow as you wait for your garden to come into balance. How do gardeners manage in the meantime?

If a little bit of benign neglect doesn't do the trick, I next turn to timing my plantings to avoid the worst insect problems. I mentioned in chapter 2 how I use timing to keep cabbageworm problems to a minimum, by planting early in the spring and late in the fall when the butterflies aren't out and about. I also have good luck keeping carrot flies at bay by harvesting crops at the first sign of wilting leaves. Below, I'll regale you with two more examples of using planting time to outwit pests.

Squash Vine Borers

Squash vine borers were my archnemesis during our early years homesteading, so much so that I even resorted to spraying Bt on the plants' stems. (Okay, pictures don't lie—I made my husband do the spraying.) And I'm glad to say that the Bt *didn't* help. Why am I glad? Because if that seemingly innocuous spray had proven effective, I might never have figured out less intrusive ways to keep vine borers in check.

Variety selection was part of my solution, as I'll explain in the next chapter. But the biggest reason I started being able to harvest summer squash is because I learned to succession plant these speedy vegetables biweekly in the summer garden. In zone

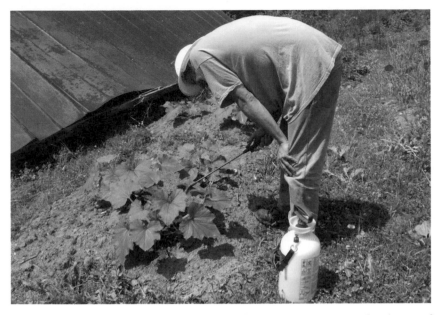

Our first approach to squash-vine-borer control was spraying Bt. Visit the glossary for more information about this and other chemicals mentioned in the text.

6 (last frost: May 15, first frost: October 10), I planted crookneck (summer) squash on May 1 (a gamble), May 15, June 1, June 15, and July 1 (a slight gamble), a schedule that overwhelmed us with tasty squashes despite heavy vine-borer pressure and with the use of no other control measures beyond variety selection.

Yes, the bad bugs moved in and killed our squash plants eventually, but not until after I'd collected at least a few big harvests from each bed. By the time the earliest vines start failing, I had another planting of summer squash just waiting to take their place. Meanwhile, I could rip out the infected plants and put the debris in the chicken coop so my garden didn't turn into a breeding ground for vine borers.

I highly recommend this method to all organic growers battling vine borers, but northern growers should take special notice. In their colder climate, vine borers have only a single generation per year, meaning that if these gardeners wait to plant their squash until after the vine borers lay their eggs, late plantings of squash will be pristine.

Succession planting is handy with other types of vegetables as well, although the strategy only works if you choose varieties that put out a big harvest right away. For example, I succession plant bush beans rather than growing runner beans since the former provide lots of green beans before the bean beetles move in to dine, and I also succession plant cucumbers in order to beat cucumber beetles and bacterial wilt. On the other hand, succession planting wouldn't be a good choice for tomatoes or peppers since even determinate varieties require months of growth before they ripen their first fruit.

Another benefit of succession planting comes when the food reaches our table. A few studies have suggested that cucurbits (and perhaps other vegetables) have more micronutrients on hand when they mature their first fruits, so the earliest harvest often tastes best. Some gourmet farmers pull out their squash vines after the first picking as a matter of course, figuring it's better to maximize flavor rather than yield. So maybe the borers are trying to do us a favor by prompting us to eat the most nutrient-rich and tasty vegetables possible.

Cicadas

I learned my next lesson on timing the hard way. In 2012, periodic cicadas crawled out of the ground in our area and regaled us with their ocean-like symphony. I was intrigued by the natural occurrence and enjoyed feeding these protein-rich insects to our chickens, so at first I thought the

Female cicadas lay their eggs on the twigs of young fruit trees, creating extensive scars.

Brian Cooper shared these photos of cicada killer wasps "taking cicadas right out of the air."

periodic cicadas were a boon to our farm. Then I saw the damage pictured on page 32.

It turns out that cicadas lay their eggs in tender twigs of young trees and seem to preferentially choose fruiting species over wild saplings. When the young cicadas hatch from their twig homes, the nymphs drop to the ground and tunnel down to feed on the tree's roots. While the root sucking may be a long-term problem, the real issue is that the nymphs damage fruit-tree twigs so much while coming out of their eggs that the branches often break off and die.

Of course, even cicadas have natural predators, but the insects' periodic nature is designed to keep predation to a minimum. Cicada killers and other animals that preferentially feed on cicadas can only survive at low population levels most of the time since their food is scarce. Every thirteen to seventeen years, the adult periodic cicadas come out of the ground and provide a feast. But by then, the predator levels are so low that the majority of the cicadas survive untouched. That's why we have to get a bit more wily when dealing with these insects—periodic cicadas have outwitted their natural enemies and we can't count on help from nature.

The short-term solution to cicada damage is to net adult cicadas away from twigs as soon as you hear periodic cicadas calling. But smarter orchardists also plan around cicada cycles. If you go to hydrodictyon.eeb.uconn.edu/projects/cicada/databases /magicicada/magi_search.php, you can choose your state and county then find out when periodic cicadas have emerged in your region recently. Add the appropriate number of years to those emergence dates and you'll know when the next brood will be out looking for baby fruit trees.

In a perfect world, you'd plant fruit trees no more than two years before cicada-emergence dates since cicadas aren't as interested in older trees. Smart orchardists also choose not to winter-prune fruit trees during a year when periodic cicadas are due to emerge, knowing the cicadas will do some of the pruning job for them. That's true permaculture gardening at work!

Chapter 5:
Helping Plants
Resist Insects

After timing I often turn to variety selection, companion planting, and proper plant nutrition to reduce insect pressure in the garden. In fact, choosing resistant fruit and vegetable varieties is my favorite low-work method of insect control in our own plot.

Resistant Varieties

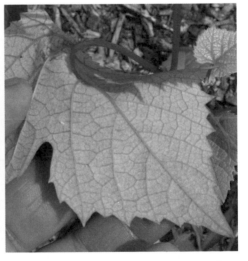

Japanese beetles enjoy eating the leaves of French hybrid grapes.

American grapes have thicker leaves with whitened undersides and tend to be less favored by hungry Japanese beetles.

Japanese beetles taught me my first lesson about variety selection. We had a terrible problem with these invasive beetles on our grapevines until I realized that French-hybrid grapes are much more tasty to Japanese beetles than are American varieties. The latter can be distinguished by their thicker leaves, which are often whitened underneath, and by the relative paucity of beetles chowing down on the leaves. In addition to grapes, Japanese beetles also defoliated our young sweet-cherry tree, but damage on other plants seemed to stay at low enough levels that the trees could shrug it off. After switching our small vineyard over to American grapes and removing our cherry tree, the Japanese beetle pressure was reduced to the point where hand-picking was sufficient to keep beetles at bay.

In general, variety selection can be a helpful strategy in controlling at least five of the dirty-dozen worst garden pests in the U.S. The table opposite lists pest-resistant varieties drawn from several different extension-service websites and other sources.

Butternut squash resists pests that kill other cucurbits, making the species an excellent low-work crop for the beyond-organic gardener.

Cabbage varieties with dark green leaves are usually the most resistant to cabbageworms.

Pest insect	Insect-resistant varieties
Cabbageworms	Collards, Brussels sprouts, broccoli, and cabbage are tastier to these insects than are other crucifers. Within each type of vegetable, vegetables with dark green, glossy leaves are more resistant to cabbageworms, while cabbage butterflies sometimes avoid laying eggs on red cabbage varieties. Resistant cabbage varieties include Chieftain Savoy, Early Globe, Mammoth, Red Acre, Red Rock, Round Dutch, and Savoy Perfection Drumhead.
Corn earworms	Any corn with a tight husk will be more resistant to earworms. Specifically resistant varieties include Country Gentlemen, Golden Security, Seneca, Silvergent, and Staygold.
Cucumber beetles	In general, cucumber beetles prefer zucchini-type squash over others and don't like burpless cucumbers as well as other varieties. Ashley, Chipper, Gemini, Piccadilly, Poinsett, and Stono cucumbers; Blue Hubbard, Early Prolific, Scallop, Straightneck, and White Bush squash; and Galia, Passport, Pulsar, Rising Star, and Super Star melons are all reported to be resistant to cucumber beetles.

However, the more important issue is to select a variety resistant to the bacterial wilt carried by cucumber beetles. These wilt-resistant varieties include Connecticut Yellow Field, Harvest Moon, and Howden pumpkins; Waltham butternut; Buttercup squash; Black Beauty zucchini; and Ashley, Chinese Long, Chipper, County Fair, Eversweet, Gemini, Improved Long Green, Saticoy Hybrid, Sunnybrook, and Tokyo Long cucumbers. Most watermelon varieties are resistant to bacterial wilt. |
| Squash bugs | Squash bugs prefer yellow summer squash over zucchinis, squash over pumpkins, pumpkins over gourds, and gourds over melons. Resistant varieties include acorn squash, butternuts, Early Summer Crookneck, Green Striped Cushaw, Improved Green Hubbard, Spaghetti, Sweet Cheese, and zucchinis (except for the susceptible Cocozelle). |
| Squash vine borers | Varieties resistant to squash vine borers tend to have thin, tough stems. In addition, vining types are more resistant than bush types since the former can root along their nodes and thus survive moderate levels of borer damage. The most resistant varieties include butternuts and Green Striped Cushaw, followed by Dickenson Pumpkin and Summer Crookneck. Other varieties reputed to have at least some resistance include acorn squash, Cucuzzi (also known as snake gourd), and Connecticut Field, Dickenson, and Small Summer pumpkins. |

Companion Planting

Companion planting is a bit like choosing resistant vegetable varieties, but you instead plant the varieties you want and then cozy up a more toxic (from an insect's point of view) plant beside your favored crop. For example, some gardeners believe that interplanting basil with tomatoes will keep hornworms at bay. My experience with companion planting has been largely negative since I find that plants need to be very close together to get any insect-repelling effect, at which point you see competition between the vegetable you're trying to grow and its companion.

Hoverflies like this one are attracted to nectar sources in the garden, and their larvae stick around to eat aphids and caterpillars.

Agricultural scientists agree that most companion planting isn't going to provide any pest-control help for the backyard gardener. However, a few interplanting mixtures do seem to work. Trap crops (as I'll discuss in chapter 8) can be used to draw insect pests away from your main crop, and flowers near your vegetables will definitely attract beneficial insects. (See chapter 11 for suggestions on which flowers to plant.) In addition, the roots of African and French marigolds have been shown to emit a chemical that repels nematodes (a type of microorganism that can harm roots), although you'll get the most bang for your buck by planting marigolds as a cover crop then killing the bed of flowers shortly before planting your nematode-sensitive crop. Finally, at least one source suggests that corn planted amid your

A diverse garden attracts pollinators and confuses pests.

squash plants may confuse squash vine borers looking for a spot to lay their eggs.

Although I pooh-pooh most types of companion planting, I do feel that a diverse garden will fare much better than a monoculture when treated organically. On my own homestead, I break the ground up into permanent beds about three feet wide and anywhere from five to twenty feet long. Except for corn (which has to be grown in large blocks for wind-pollination purposes), I plant each type of vegetable in several different places around the garden, so a bed of cucumbers might be surrounded by beans, tomatoes, and Swiss chard rather than by the other cucumbers I'm growing that year. This patchwork-quilt garden gives me many of the benefits of companion planting without requiring the extra work of dealing with species mixtures all in the same bed. (On the downside, my technique does make planning the garden rotation more complicated. But they say puzzles are good for fending off Alzheimer's, right?)

Plant Nutrition

The last facet of outwitting insects is to make your garden less susceptible to insect infestations by keeping your plants healthy. I already touched on this issue briefly in chapter 2 when I mentioned that many aphid problems can be traced back to overfertilization of the plants being consumed. A related problem occurs with green beans—bean beetles can't digest the form of nitrogen created in nitrogen-fixing nodules in the plants' roots, but the beetles love the form of nitrogen that the plants suck up directly from compost (or from other fertilizers) in the soil. So one way to keep bean beetles in check is to skip topdressing any garden area where you plan to grow beans that year, forcing the plants to create all of their own nitrogen from scratch.

On a related note, many organic gardeners will tell you that every insect infestation is linked to a nutritional deficiency in the plant. While this idea has intuitive appeal, I've yet to find any solid data to back the hypothesis up. On the other hand, a well-nourished plant is likely to provide more nutrient-dense food for the table, so there's no reason not to provide the best possible nutrition for your vegetables. Applying organic amendments like compost and mulch will probably do the job for you, especially if you mix things up and draw your organic matter from different sources each year. If you want to be scientific, a soil test is a good way to get a handle on any potential deficiencies, at which point you can apply rock dusts or other amendments to boost mineral levels into the recommended range.

Keeping the soil balanced and plants healthy is something I do as a matter of course, but there are times when I put more energy into the campaign than usual. If a new insect problem pops up and doesn't respond to any of my usual control techniques, that's a good time to start researching nutrient deficiencies. For example, I was tipped off to the bean problem mentioned earlier because many of my bean beds were overrun with beetles but

If you keep the nitrogen levels in your soil low, you won't see many Mexican bean beetles. Instead, minor pests like this broad-headed bug (*Alydus eurinus*) will show up to suck juices out of the seeds.

the beans I'd planted into not-very-decomposed rye stubble were virtually untouched. The rye stubble was locking up nitrogen from the compost I'd applied to the soil, which in turn required the bean plants to kick their rhizobial bacteria into gear to create homegrown nitrogen for the plant. If you keep your eyes open for similar scenarios in which one bed of a vegetable is untouched while its neighbors are overrun, you'll soon discover which deficiencies or excesses may be at work in your own garden.

Chapter 6:
Physical Barriers

L ow-key methods of fending off pest insects, unfortunately, only go so far. If you'd rather not dive directly into hand-picking and pesticides, one option involves simply blocking the offending insects out.

Physical barriers between pest insects and their prey can include greenhouses, row covers, or (on the backyard scale) simply growing your vegetables in pots. I'll start with the last, which I've found particularly handy for keeping flea beetles away from the tender leaves of baby eggplants.

Potted Plants

If you asked me a year ago why I didn't grow eggplants, I could have answered in two words—flea beetles. These tiny insects nibble on several different types of vegetables, but only young eggplants are so tasty that the flea beetles deeply harm the plant. In fact, unprotected eggplants often succumb to flea-beetle depredations long before they're able to set fruit.

Flea beetles aren't a major problem on most vegetables, but they do tend to kill eggplants in our area.

On the large scale, organic farmers often keep flea beetles away from their eggplants using row covers like the ones I'll describe in the next section. But row covers have their own range of problems and my one attempt at keeping eggplants alive beneath the permeable fabric dramatically failed.

But then I started thinking. Flea beetles overwinter in the soil and pop up fully formed and ready to eat the following spring. It's this early feasting that destroys eggplants' long-term vigor . . . so what if I broke the cycle by getting rid of the infested dirt?

Of course, plants require soil. But they don't necessarily have to be set out directly in the ground. So instead of putting my eggplants in the main garden soon after our frost-free

On a small scale, eggplants can be grown in pots for a few months until they're strong enough to withstand flea-beetle infestations.

date, I instead transplanted them into one- and two-gallon pots. Then I kept the youngsters on a folding table outside my back door where I'd remember to water them frequently . . . and, incidentally, where flea beetles were unlikely to invade.

Feeding the young vegetables with potting soil instead of garden soil meant that no flea beetles erupted from dormancy in my eggplants' immediate vicinity. A few flea beetles *did* find them after a while, but the holes in the leaves were few and far between. And by the time the plants were three months old and outgrowing their planters, their leaves were far less tender and unlikely to succumb to flea-beetle depredations. For the first time ever, I enjoyed an organic eggplant harvest with very little work.

In addition to saving the lives of eggplants, this same method can be used to counteract several other soil-borne plant pests. Cutworms, for example, are caterpillars that live in the dirt and love beheading young vegetables of many types, particularly tomatoes, broccoli, and corn. Similarly, overwintering adult cucumber beetles decimate cucurbit seedlings in some areas while slugs hide under mulches and can quickly consume their favorite baby plants. In all cases, starting seeds inside and holding back seedlings until they're past their danger threshold can make pest-insect damage a thing of the past.

Row Covers

Quick hoops used to protect summer crops from pest insects don't need to be nearly as structurally complicated as winter quick hoops required to stand up against wind and snow. The only essential feature is that the edges be weighed down thoroughly so no insects can sneak inside.

Potted plants are too time-consuming for the large-scale grower, but row covers fill in where pots leave off. Simply put, row covers are any type of permeable fabric used to maintain warmth in the winter and fend off pests in the summer, the fabric in question being either draped directly atop your plants or held erect using quick hoops. (See *The Weekend Homesteader* for tips on creating quick hoops that will stand up to wind and storms.) Since row-cover fabric allows light and rain to pass through to some extent, it doesn't have to be vented like plastic. And if you carefully weigh down all edges with soil, no insects will find their way inside.

Which bad bugs can be fended off using row covers? Classics include aphids, army worms, cabbageworms, carrot flies, Colorado potato beetles, cucumber beetles, flea beetles, grasshoppers, Japanese beetles, leaf miners, root maggots, squash bugs, and squash vine borers. Row covers can also deter depredations of bigger nibblers like rabbits, groundhogs, and deer.

When using row covers to exclude pest insects, it's essential that you find a way to weigh down all of the edges of the fabric and that you cover the plants from the start so no pest insects will find their way inside the protected tent. Some pests, like flea beetles and cucumber beetles, spend part of their life cycle in the soil, so you'll need to use proper crop rotation to ensure the inesects aren't already in your ground before you put a row cover in place. Otherwise you'll be trapping pest insects around your plants rather than blocking the bad bugs out.

Another tricky part about using row covers is ensuring that fruit-setting plants are properly pollinated. On the pollination front, you obviously don't have to worry if you're growing a crop—like lettuce, broccoli, or potatoes—for the leaves, flower buds, or roots. But if you want fruits on your squashes and eggplants, you'll need to find a way for the pollinators to get inside.

Many gardeners simply remove their row covers and return to hand-picking pests once plants hit the bloom stage. After all, young crops are often the most sensitive to insect damage, so this technique will be sufficient for eggplants (less so for cucumbers and squash). When dealing with cucurbits, you might choose to hand pollinate with a paintbrush, keeping the row cover off for such a brief period in the process that few pest insects find a way inside.

The other big issue with row covers is heat stress, a problem I discovered firsthand when I got clever and decided to keep cabbageworms away from young Brussels sprouts using summer quick hoops. There are various types of row-cover fabric, but even the thinnest holds in at least some warmth and creates a greenhouse-type environment underneath. In the winter, this is a bonus. During July, the heat retention can mean the death knell of sensitive plants.

Luckily, other materials exist that can be used atop plants who can't stand hot weather. Shade netting is silver and reflective—a good choice for cool-weather crops that would have preferred skipping summer altogether. Meanwhile, insect netting is an extremely permeable barrier, a good choice for summer-loving crops. Finally, garden writer Barbara Pleasant offers another suggestion—skip the garden center entirely and instead head to the craft shop for wedding dress tulle.

No matter which type of fabric you choose for your row covers, I have one final suggestion for preventing disasters beneath quick hoops—lift up an edge and peek inside at least once a week.. Summer crops grown beneath row covers might need more frequent watering and could build up pests that snuck in before the barrier went into place. In a busy garden, it's easy to forget about plantings that are out of sight and out of mind. Don't cover up your eggplants to protect them then lose the crop due to neglect!

Pests under Cover

In 1984, Kip Rondy bought an old Ohio dairy farm, regulated out of business, denuded of trees, and heavily hayed to within an inch of its life. Thirty-four years later, he and his wife Becky make a living for themselves and a heaping handful of employees on the rechristened Green Edge Gardens (www.greenedgegardens.com), named for the trees that now cover both hillsides and shelter the fifteen-acre growing zone on the valley's floor.

Between a CSA, wholesale runs to the nearest city, and a thriving farmer's market presence in nearby towns, Green Edge feeds

(continued)

The land that would later become Greenedge Gardens, circa 1950.

hundreds of customers every week. They grow microgreens and mushrooms in specially designed and repurposed buildings and harvest row crops from their fields. Still, the heart of the operation and the garden's most visible aspect involves ten unheated high tunnels that extend the garden season throughout the winter months.

Using a system developed by Green Edge of special row covers and plastic sheeting beneath each high tunnel, Kip and Becky are able to not only hold over fall greens through the winter, they promote active growth of lettuces and a wide variety of leafy greens all winter long. Unfortunately, extending the gardening season to last through the winter months comes with its own set of problems. Insects move in to nibble when predators are dormant, and sometimes extremely cold temperatures coupled with cloud cover can make harvesting tricky. Nonetheless, years of experience have taught them how to bring in the harvest despite these conditions.

The most notable pest problems in Green Edge's high tunnels are aphids and mites, which can have devastating effects on overwintering greens. And while Kip and Becky are willing to resort

Greenedge Gardens in 2018.

to the occasional organic pesticide, they more frequently dispel insect invaders with classic "bug murders." In other words, they hand-pick.

Don't think you can hand-pick aphids and mites? Of course you can—just harvest the entire plant! Since Green Edge Gardens is set up with a health-department-approved vegetable-washing room, heavily infested greens get triple-rinsed, go into the industrial-strength salad spinners, then come out the other side pristine and ready to eat.

Meanwhile, a fallow season once every three years (or more often if harvests go down) keeps the entire greenhouse ecosystem in balance. During each high tunnel's summer off, the farmers remove the plastic so that rain can wash salts out of the soil then they plant cover crops into the vacant land. In addition to cleaning and revigorating the soil, good insects move in at the same time to chase pest insects away.

While you may not plan to build high tunnels any time soon, the theory for pest control beneath quick hoops in the home garden or in an attached sunroom is remarkably similar. Remaining vigilant and catching the first few bad bugs before they expand will nip potential infestations in the bud. Meanwhile, opening up your covered growing area to the wild will make the protected pockets much less amenable to aphids and other tender-footed pests when

(continued)

The last row of spring lettuce remains in a high tunnel turned fallow for the summer.

the weather is mild. After all, just because you're growing under cover doesn't mean you can't take advantage of the beneficial insect populations you've built up in the garden outside!

Chapter 7:
Hand-Picking

Ihope the previous chapters didn't make you think that keeping bad bugs in check is as simple as sitting on the porch and watching the wildlife eat them up. Sure, some of that happens, but there are times when the gardener needs to step in and keep things in line. When that time comes, my first line of defense is hand-picking.

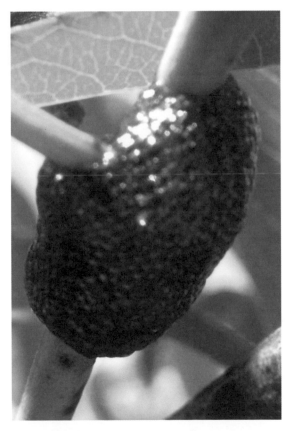

If you catch them early, tent caterpillars are easy to hand-pick. Initially, you can greatly reduce tent-caterpillar populations by removing egg cases while pruning your fruit trees over the winter.

After tent-caterpillar eggs hatch, the cobwebby homes of the larvae are also easy to pull out of low branches.

How to Pick Bugs

I deter imminent population explosions in my garden primarily through hand-picking. While this sounds like I've retreated to the Dark Ages, I assure you that I can hit all of the problematic spots in an acre-plus garden in less than ten minutes. The trick is to pick during the cool of the morning when insects are sluggish, to pick often (three times a week at the minimum), and to know which problematic insects are likely to be in which spot at which time. It's also handy to understand that beetles tend to drop directly down when startled. So if you hold a cup of water beneath their resting place, you can "pick" these fliers without touching anything with your bare hands.

Various sources will tell you to knock bad insects into a container of soapy water or gasoline, but I use plain water in a straight-sided jar or cup. The insects almost never clamber back out, and by keeping my liquid additive-free, I can dump Japanese beetles, June bugs, and cabbageworms into the chicken coop, turning bad bugs into free eggs.

Insects beyond the three listed above are likely to fly or crawl away before they're eaten by the flock, so I use those less-tasty critters to create caterpillar tea. Asparagus beetles, bean beetles, and tent caterpillars all die within a few hours when left in a cup of water. Then the nutrient-rich broth can be poured around the roots of hungry plants just before I start picking the next day's invaders.

Alternatively, the less squeamish can skip a step by squishing pest insects in the field. Blog reader Dave Miller adds slugs to his hand-picking campaign, snipping the slimy nibblers in half with scissors whenever he catches them in his garden. Similarly, I squeeze to death caterpillars too young to pick easily, along with various types of insect eggs. Just make sure you're killing all pests rather than just knocking them off the plants in question—a bug murder is only successful once your victim is dead.

Picking by the Calendar

In general, if you're fast enough to catch them, all pest insects can be hand-picked. The trick is to hit them early before populations get out of control. I find it handy to mark on my calendar when major infestations (like Japanese beetles) are likely to arise so that I can nip them in the bud. After all, the earliest Japanese beetles to emerge from the soil emit pheromones that attract others to their dining rooms. So if you catch the first beetles to congregate on your beloved plants and remove them, chances are the biggest party will set up shop in the weeds instead of in your berry patch.

Even for insects that don't congregate in this manner, if you kill the first to arrive then each early-bird won't be able to reproduce and turn into twenty or a hundred pests later in the year. That's why it might be worth pulling out plantings (like buggy beans) on which the pests have reached critical mass in the interest of keeping pest populations low throughout the garden. And that's also why it's so important to hand-pick with regularity, since daily (or at least thrice-weekly) pickings will keep insect populations at a dull roar.

Chapter 8:
Trap Crops

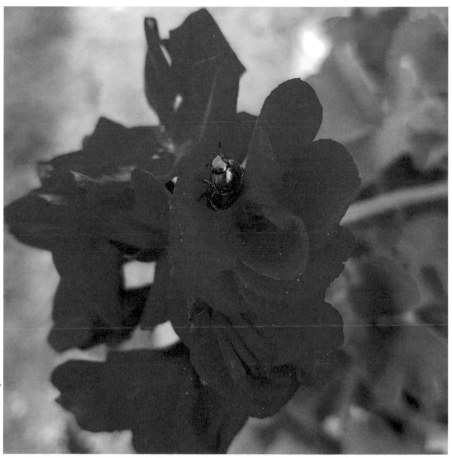

Geraniums not only attract Japanese beetles, a chemical in the petals also stuns the beetles long enough so they become easy pickings for predators.

Some gardeners take hand-picking to another level by growing trap crops—plants that pest insects prefer over the variety the gardener wants for herself. The theory is simple. You set out the trap crop, wait for bugs to show up, then kill the pests with one of the methods outlined below.

What counts as a trap crop? Bug attractants can involve an early planting of the same variety you intend to grow for your main crop, or they can be a tastier (from an insect's point of view) variety that you plant beside the row intended for your plate. The table below suggests several proven trap-crop varieties you might want to try in your own plot.

Plants used as trap crops	
Pest to be attracted	Trap crops
Cabbage root flies	Chinese cabbage, collards, and radishes
Cabbageworms	Collards
Carrot root flies	Garlic, medic, onions
Colorado potato beetles	Horseradish, Superior potatoes (and pre-sprouted potatoes of other varieties that will come up before the main crop), tansy, Vittoria eggplant
Cucumber beetles	Baby Blue Hubbard squash, nasturtiums, and New England Hubbard squash
Flea beetles	Chinese cabbage, collards, nasturtiums, radishes, Vittoria eggplant
Harlequin bugs	Southern Giant Curled mustard
Japanese beetles	*Pelargonium × hortorum* geraniums. (Unlike other trap crops, these geraniums not only attract Japanese beetles, they also paralyze and kill the pests.)
Leaf-footed beetles	Sorghum variety NK300 and Peredovik-type sunflowers
Pepper maggot flies	Hot cherry peppers
Slugs	Chervil, French marigolds, and sorrel
Squash vine borers	Nasturtiums
Stink bugs	Black-eyed peas, buckwheat, millet, sesbania, sorghum, sunflowers, and triticale
Tomato hornworms	Dill and lovage

How to Utilize Trap Crops

Trap cropping methodology varies greatly depending on whether you're trying to protect a ten-acre pepper field or are doting over a single raised bed in your backyard. I'll cover both types of situations below just in case.

We'll start with planting arrangements. In large fields, your best bet is to set out a rectangle of trap crops completely surrounding the vegetable to be harvested since this buffer can prevent pest insects from making their way into the heart of the commercial planting. In contrast, on the backyard scale, your goal should simply be for the trap crop to be located in close proximity to the planting you want to protect.

Either way, vigilance is paramount. The insects that come to your trap crop won't just hang out there and ignore nearby plantings—they have to be killed before they can breed. Hand-picking is a classic solution, while those more squeamish may turn to insecticidal sprays. Alternatively, if you're trapping an insect that tends to arrive all at once (like cucumber beetles or Japanese beetles), you can pull out the entire trap crop and dispose of it within a sealed compost bin. In a few cases, flame weeders might be equally effective at frying both the trap crop and the associated insects. Either way, the goal is to kill all of the bad bugs at once so nearby crops stay pristine.

A Horseradish Cautionary Tale

Ask anyone at Athens, Ohio's Westside Community Gardens about bad bugs and they'll point fingers at the harlequin bug. This colorful stink-bug relative has been only a minor inconvenience in my own plots, so I found myself scratching my head over the gardeners' heated tirades. Was I missing something? Had harlequin bugs turned into top-ten garden pests while I was looking the other way?

Harlequin bugs (*Murgantia histrionica*) are usually only a problem on cruciferous crops like cabbages and broccoli. But when their populations explode, they willingly nibble on many other garden plants.

The story, it turns out, is different than I'd originally imagined. It began with a gardener who possessed such a deep-seated love for horseradish that he filled his entire plot with this tenacious perennial herb. The plants were striking, the condiments were delicious . . . then the harlequin bugs moved in.

It turns out that harlequins like nothing better than horseradish leaves, but horseradish makes a terrible trap crop. The vertical, slippery leaves are perfect for sliding down and evading gardener fingers, and the horseradish aficionado didn't particularly care for squishing bugs anyway.

So the harlequin-bug populations soared on the lazy gardener's horseradish . . . and the bugs soon had to seek out less favored foods. Harlequins prefer crucifers because those plants' mustardy flavor can be secreted away inside the insects, making the latter unpalatable to birds. But once harlequin bugs run out of horseradish, they willingly move on to other options. Soon, nearby plots had become overwhelmed by the marauders, with harlequins nibbling every crop in the community garden to within an inch of its life.

The takeaway message from this anecdote is simple and applicable to anyone's garden patch. If you ignore trap crops, they become insect nurseries instead. So don't be Horseradish Guy— take care of those congregations of pest insects before they take care of your crops.

Stumbling Upon Natural Trap Crops

Photo credit: Leigh Tate.

Cucumber beetles are attracted to wild amaranth in Leigh Tate's garden.

Leigh Tate, gardener, homesteader, blogger, and author of *Prepper's Livestock Handbook* and *5 Acres & A Dream the Book* shared the following anecdote about her own path toward trap cropping.

"My introduction to insect trap plants was quite by accident. Wild amaranth grows readily in my part of the country and usually I keep it pulled. One year, however, I got behind in weeding and had a number of wild amaranth plants growing in the garden. I was surprised to discover that they were quite appealing to cucumber beetles. So much so, that I had far less cucumber beetle damage that year than previously. Who knew insects had favorites? Since then I have allowed several wild amaranths to grow every summer to attract those cucumber beetles. I know right where to find them and can remove them by hand for damage control.

"Unlike deterrents which repel insect pests, trap plants actually attract those same pests and draw them away from the veggies I don't want damaged. Since that first accidental experience, I've learned about a number of trap plants that help with my particular gardening problems: dill for tomato hornworms, zinnias and geraniums for Japanese beetles, sunflowers for stink bugs, and chervil and coleus for slugs. I've read that aphids love nasturtiums, but my summers are often too hot and dry to keep nasturtiums happy. Instead I've been experimenting with alternatives for aphids such as mustard and sunflowers. These might not be as effective as nasturtiums, but if they work in my climate, then they are still of benefit to me.

"The trap plants I've listed are not only effective at insect control, but beautiful too. This appeals to my mixed companion bed style of gardening. One consideration, however, is that if the decoys are planted in or close to the beds they are meant to protect, then it's only a hop or short crawl for hungry pests to reach the original target plant. Many gardeners find it more effective to plant the decoys around the periphery of the garden. I have found this to be true as well. My wild amaranth grows nowhere near my cucumbers but attracts those beetles very well."

Chapter 9:
Chemical Shortcuts

So you've taken the high road, you've tried hand picking and row covers, but your garden looks more like a rag doll than like a productive patch. What's the solution now?

In the first edition of this book, I skipped most mention of pesticides. After all, I don't use them in my own garden. Why should I recommend problematic products to you?

But the reality is that if your crop fails, you'll end up buying replacement food at the grocery store or farmer's market. And every large-scale producer, whether conventional or

Photo credit: Brian Cooper.

Chemical use in the garden is a balancing act that is often just as likely to kill predators—like this cannibal fly—as pests.

organic, understands that sometimes you have to spray to bring home the harvest. So, without further ado, here are some tips on conventional pesticides that pass the organic test.

Soap and Water

Okay, I really *am* going to recommend off-the-shelf chemicals shortly. But first, I want to make a plug for water—approved by even beyond-organic gardeners like me.

"Water? That's not an insecticide!" you're probably thinking. Okay, hold on a minute and hear me out.

A few insects—notably aphids and whiteflies—are so tiny that all it takes is one good thunderstorm to wash them so far away from your plants that they have no hope of latching back on. Which means that plants safely protected from storms on your window ledge or in your greenhouse may build up populations of pests that would never make it in the great outdoors.

The solution? A nice hard spray from a garden hose or kitchen faucet can often get rid of an aphid or whitefly infestation before it gets too bad. Just be sure to keep the flow moderate enough so you don't injure the plant. Now that's a type of spray even I will gladly use!

If water isn't enough to do the trick, you might turn next to insecticidal soaps. These relatively innocuous products are similar to the soaps used in your kitchen but are formulated to be more plant friendly and at the same time more problematic to pests.

What can you kill with soaps? These mild insecticides work by covering up the holes insects use to breathe and by creeping through the insects' skins to directly harm their cells. As a result, only soft-bodied insects like aphids, lace bugs, mealybugs, mites, psyllids, scale (when young), thrips, and whiteflies are affected. Hard-shelled beetles are immune.

As with any type of chemical, however, soaps come with a few warnings. First, soap *will* kill soft-bodied beneficials just as easily as they kill similar pest species. And insecticidal soaps don't kill any bugs that show up after the initial treatment, so you'll need to keep reapplying as new insects colonize the soaped-up plant.

The other concern with soaps comes in relation to the plants themselves. Even assuming you carefully steer clear of detergents (which are bad for plant leaves), insecticidal soaps can cause allergic reactions in certain types of plants. Cucumbers are the only vegetable reputed to be thoroughly anti-soap, but flowers of other types of fruits and vegetables can be harmed by the sudsy spray. Meanwhile, stressed plants of all sorts are likely to react negatively to soap application, as are plants treated during hot, sunny days. If in doubt, treat a small area and keep an eye out for yellow or brown leaf spotting during the next twenty-four hours before choosing to spray your entire patch.

All of that said, insecticidal soaps are one of the safest organic pesticides on the market. Just be sure to buy products intended for garden use, apply no more often than once or twice a week, and dilute concentrates with rainwater or other soft water if your tap is full of calcium. Following those instructions, you're not likely to go too far wrong using soap.

Traps

Flypaper is the classic sticky trap. Here, the glue-coated surface is being used to control fungus gnats in a mushroom fruiting area.

Physical or chemical traps are another type of garden shortcut that are unlikely to cause negative effects in your plot. The theory is simple—pests are attracted to a scent or a color, then they either drown or become stuck to a flypaper-like surface on which they perish. The primary downsides are cost and fiddlyness— you'll need to refresh traps relatively frequently to maintain their efficacy within the garden. Environmental repercussions, on the other hand, are minimal.

I'll begin with the least useful type of trap—pheromone traps. I mentioned these previously in the Japanese beetle section, but let me expand upon them slightly here. A pheromone is simply a scent that animals release into the air to communicate with others of their species. In the insect world, pheromones are precursors to sex, attracting males to a female ready to mate.

So how is that useful in your garden? Scientists have figured out how to isolate and recreate pheromones of various species, so you can mimic the scent of a sexy female and draw in herds of starry-eyed males. While these traps only target the gentlemen of the species and thus won't eradicate entire populations, they can be handy for monitoring when the first pest insects arrive in the spring.

Sticky traps are in higher demand by the home gardener because they capture both males and females indiscriminately. These simple traps consist of a piece of colored plastic covered by a substance like Tanglefoot that makes interested insects stick tight. You can either buy sticky traps ready-made, or can purchase a bottle of glue to coat homemade traps of various sorts.

Once again, sticky traps see the most use as monitoring equipment, especially in greenhouses where yellow cards can give managers an idea when pest populations are about to explode. Placement of cards is of prime importance in this scenario—always close to preferred host plants but in various orientations and locations depending on which type of insect is meant to be trapped. For example, fungus gnats are best caught with horizontal sticky cards placed just above the soil surface, while sticky cards close to the crop canopy work better for thrips.

But can't you just use sticky cards like flypaper to get rid of all the pests? Red sticky balls (or Red Delicious apples) covered with Tanglefoot are often used to great effect by organic orcharders intent upon trapping apple maggots while the real apples on the tree are still young. Beyond that example, however, large-scale use of sticky traps for pest eradication runs into several hurdles difficult to overcome.

First comes sheer labor. Sticky traps need to be changed out once or twice a week, which either means purchasing a new premade trap (pricey) or removing and reapplying the Tanglefoot coating from the existing trap. In many cases, sticky traps have to be located only a few feet apart for full coverage. And perhaps more daunting from an ecosystem perspective is the tendency of these traps to catch pollinators who mistake the bright colors for a nectar-rich flower. Parasitic wasps are also often found on yellow sticky traps, meaning that your hornworm population may explode even as your winged aphid infestation declines.

Moving on from pheremone and sticky traps, let's consider a DIY trap that's easy to make at home—beer traps for slugs. This old standby consists of taking any shallow dish, filling it partway up with beer, then waiting for the slugs to move in and die. According to a *Mother Earth News* survey, beer traps are 80 percent effective at trapping slugs . . . but what kind of slug do they catch?

Interestingly, many gardeners report that it's the fermentation that slugs are attracted to, not the beer itself. So you can get just as good results by using bread yeast mixed with warm water and sugar to produce a yeasty scent similar to that found in a can of beer.

Which raises a conundrum—if the slugs are being drawn to fermentation, are they really herbivores that graze upon garden leaves? Or are the slugs being drowned instead the beneficial species that help decompose organic matter . . . which is often being worked upon by fungi and thus has a yeasty scent?

Now that I've rained on your parade quite thoroughly, it's time to mention the sole type of trap I would use in my own garden— shingle traps for squash bugs. No, this isn't any type of fancy, purchased product. It's merely a few roofing shingles (or a board) placed at the base of an infested squash plant. Squash bugs like to hide at night under thin objects close to the ground, so they'll congregate beneath the shingles or boards. If you head out to the garden first thing in the morning when the air is cool and the insects are slow, it's easy to lift your trap and push the napping inhabitants into a cup of water. Of course, that brings me back to my favorite type of organic insect control—yes, I am once again telling you to hand-pick.

More Potent Pesticides

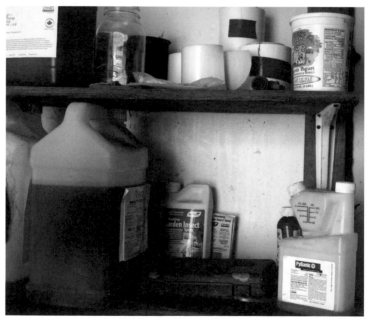

Pesticides are most organic gardeners' last resort.

Soaps and traps might not be the solution to your insect explosion, but if you need a shortcut then other organic pesticides are there to help. As with every other technique included in this chapter, I feel obliged to mention that the word "organic" doesn't mean these chemicals have no downsides. But there are times when it's better to save your crop with sprays than to give up on a harvest entirely.

There actually aren't that many types of organic pesticides on the home-garden market, so I'm going to give you a quick rundown on each. The first category is the dormant oils, which are similar to insecticidal soap. Dormant oils work via suffocation, can damage stressed plants and any type of blossom, must be reapplied frequently, and are going to kill any nearby beneficials just as efficiently as the pests you're targeting with your spray. When applied in winter or early spring to woody plants (like apple trees), though, dormant oils can help protect against aphids, mites, and scales. And they seem to be relatively innocuous to non-insects in the vicinity, which is a major plus.

Although the name is similar, neem oil operates in a different manner. Neem oil *will* smother insects just as dormant oil does upon direct contact, but the inclusion of naturally occurring azadirachtin has a longer lasting repellent effect upon any insects attempting to suck or chew on the treated plant. Most effective against insects' juvenile stages, neem oil has been shown to target aphids, beetles, caterpillars, lace bugs, leafhoppers, leaf miners, mealybugs, psyllids, thrips, and whiteflies for up to two weeks.

The close targeting of neem oil to problematic nibblers is enticing, but there is one distressing feature of the pesticide to be aware of. Neem oil is very toxic to honeybee larvae, so it's best to apply in late evening or at night after the bees have gone to bed. The goal is for most of the neem to have soaked into the plants by the time pollinators arrive the following morning, protecting honeybees from unintentionally bringing the toxic substance back to their hives.

And now, at last, it's time to address sprays like Bt (used on cabbageworms, tomato hornworms, corn earworms, European corn borers, and squash vine borers), spinosad (a broad-spectrum insecticide that kills most insects on contact), and pyrethrins (used on cabbage loopers, cucumber beetles, leafhoppers, stink bugs, and thrips) that are very much like conventional pesticides but are certified organic because they're derived from a natural source. The theory is that chemicals found naturally in the environment are less likely to harm the ecosystem or humans who eventually imbibe small quantities while chowing down on the bug-free crop. True or false?

The jury's still out on that question but is leaning toward "false." A good example is the case of rotenone, an extract from a tropical plant that started being used on organic farms in 1947. Unfortunately, more recent studies discovered that rotenone exposure results in human symptoms much like those created by Parkinson's disease, so the product is no longer allowed on shelves in the United States.

The organic pesticides currently on the market are presumed to be safer than rotenone was from a human point of view. However, most are broad-spectrum, affecting any insect they come in contact with. Meanwhile, pyrethrins, in particular, are particularly harmful to honeybees. And it's impossible to know which problematic side effects simply haven't been discovered yet.

In the end, when it comes to chemical shortcuts, you'll need to decide for yourself how daring you're willing to be. Anything that kills a bad insect is likely to kill just as many good insects. The question is—are you willing to put up with the associated loss?

Chapter 10:
Insects in the Kitchen

I'll end this boots-on-the-ground portion of the book with a discussion of insects in the kitchen. And no, I'm not talking *eating* bugs here (although I have sampled cicadas . . . and found the legs hard to get past).

So what am I talking about? If you're using natural methods of insect control, some bugs will inevitably end up on your kitchen counter, although hopefully not on your plate. This final chapter in the hands-on-control portion of the book offers some easy methods for keeping those pest insects from turning dinner into a disaster.

Debugging Your Dinner

Southern cabbageworms release their stranglehold on broccoli crowns when soaked in a bowl of warm saltwater for ten minutes.

In many cases, removing insects from your garden produce is simple. The beetles that like to hide between the gills of mushrooms drop away if you tap the cap briskly against your palm. Slugs won't hitchhike into the kitchen on your lettuce if you pick the leaves on a sunny afternoon. Oriental fruit-fly larvae (and the rotted peach centers that surround them) are simple to scoop out with a spoon after you slice the fuzzy fruits in half. And the yuckiness at the end an earworm-infected corn cob is easy to break or cut off.

When it comes right down to it, the only buggy produce I sometimes contemplate composting instead of eating is cabbageworm-infested broccoli heads. For those of you who live in the Pacific Northwest or New England—you lucked out. The rest of us risk dozens of tiny caterpillars interspersed with florets if we plant our spring broccoli too late.

Removing all of those caterpillars by hand can be daunting . . . but there *is* an easier way. Dissolve a healthy helping of salt into a bowl of warm water, cut the broccoli head into bite-size pieces, then soak the vegetables in the saltwater. After about ten minutes, nearly all of the cabbageworms will have lost their footing on the broccoli and turned into floaters within the water itself. A few good swishes and your broccoli will be nearly or completely clean . . . and this trick should work as well on any other infested produce you don't feel like hand-cleaning of bugs.

Changing Your Mindset

Unfortunately, the issue of bugs in the kitchen is more insidious than the preceding section suggests. Because many Americans don't just eschew beetles in their mushrooms; they turn up their noses at any homegrown offering that doesn't resemble the picture-perfect produce they were served during their childhood.

If you grew up on grocery-store fruits and vegetables, chances are everything you eat was sprayed with something (be it organic or not) to keep pest damage at bay. Even after that spraying, up to 20 percent of the fruits and vegetables were discarded for purely cosmetic reasons before the most beautiful specimens made their way to the supermarket shelf.

With all of this work to give the consumer perfect-looking fruits and vegetables, it's no wonder that many modern Americans look askance at twisted or insect-nibbled cucumbers from their own garden plots. In stark contrast, Gene Logsdon's *Organic Orcharding* offers a very different view of homegrown fruit. He figures that if a third of his apples are fit only for the hogs, that's

Oriental fruit fly larvae tend to infect a significant proportion of my peaches, but I've learned to simply scoop out the troubled centers and enjoy the rest of the fruit.

okay—the fruits will be turned into bacon. Another third might need to be cut up to cook into applesauce and pastries—who doesn't like apple pie? That leaves a third of his crop that is unblemished and beautiful, perfect for storing in a root cellar and nibbling on all winter long.

Looking at our home gardens in a similar manner can free us from the tyranny of perfection. If you you learn to cut out a bad spot here and there, you'll soon discover that the ugliest tomatoes really can be the tastiest ones on your plate. Similarly, many trees seem to concentrate more flavor in the bug-nibbled fruits.

Once you find yourself going out of your way to choose the uglier apple for flavor purposes then you've truly become a permaculture gardener. And that's what the final portion of this book is all about.

PART 3

A Permaculture Approach

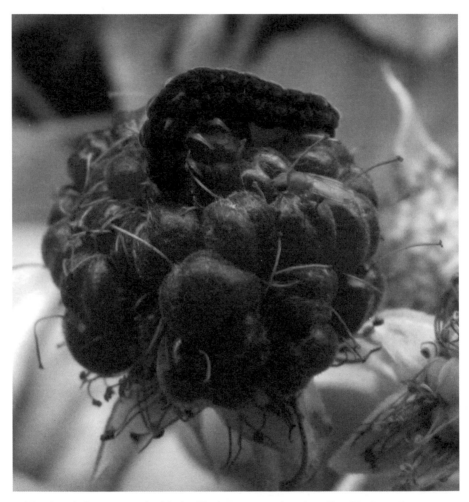

Soldier beetle larvae act a bit like bad bugs in our garden since they like to suck sugar water out of fruits. But these insects are generally beneficial because they also suck the juices out of cucumber beetles, caterpillars, grasshopper eggs, and aphids.

Chapter 11:
The Good Bugs

In the first edition of this book, I dove right into ecosystem-level insect control right up front. But I've since come to realize that, for many gardeners, balancing the garden food web is an advanced concept best broached after trap crops and hand-picking have begun to pall.

I'll start off with a quick explanation of permaculture. This gardening philosophy aims at creating self-sufficient, sustainable farms in which the larger ecosystem does some or all of the gardener's work. While it's not realistic to think that embracing permaculture will completely eliminate bad bugs in your garden, creating a balance will definitely lower your own quotient of elbow grease.

So where do you start? By realizing that not all insects in your garden are bad and by encouraging the ones that are actively doing good work. The sections that follow will give a rundown on the most important beneficial invertebrates in the average garden along with tips on how to encourage each.

Soil Workers

Nearly every invertebrate you find in the soil is a good bug with a job to do. Some (like earthworms and woodlice) digest organic matter and help build humus, while others (like centipedes and spiders) are busy eating smaller soil organisms. The combination of critters is essential for preventing the buildup of dead material on top of the soil and for releasing nutrients that plants use to grow.

On the other hand, a few soil critters are neutral or are actively bad for your garden. Ants can help disperse seeds of native

This redworm is more likely to be found in decomposing horse manure or in a worm bin than in garden soil.

plants, but they also protect aphids that suck the juices out of your trees and vegetables. Some grubs turn into Japanese beetles or June bugs (*Cotinis nitida*), the first of which eat leaves of many fruit plants and the second of which enjoy consuming the fruits themselves. And then there are the cutworms I mentioned in chapter 2—plump caterpillars who nibble the tops off seedlings.

But even problematic soil inhabitants tend to loosen the soil and to carry organic matter deep beneath the surface. Earthworms—everyone's favorite denizen of the dirt—can eat their way ten feet deep, adding nutritious calcium to everything that passes through their gut. Ants are pretty useful in this respect too since they carry food down into their nests, resulting in pockets of rich soil, while bringing mineral-rich subsoil to the surface. In wet areas (like my Virginia garden), crayfish do a similar job of nutrient movement.

A crawdad chimney is a sign that a crayfish is living in the groundwater under your garden. This type of soggy soil is best mounded up into raised beds to prevent waterlogging of plant roots.

Meanwhile, other organisms like those troublesome beetle grubs I mentioned previously fluff up soil and deposit nutrients in the form of their feces as they travel up and down through the earth. Ground-nesting bees and wasps such as sweat bees (*Halictus* sp.), miner bees (*Andrena* sp.), and various digger wasps all excavate burrows for their larvae to live in, while dung beetles fill their underground dens with rich balls of excrement. Of course, the bees, wasps, and dung beetles are all unequivocally good bugs since the first two pollinate your garden and eat bad bugs while the last help cycle nutrients through the ecosystem.

If you'd like a closer look at the critters who live beneath the surface, I recommend *Life in the Soil*, by James B. Nardi. On the other hand, if you just want to keep your garden healthy, it's pretty simple to promote life in the earth. Most soil organisms need damp ground, so topping your garden off with mulch is a great way to keep the critters active during hot summers. The use of cover crops and compost is also recommended since both will jumpstart your soil ecosystem by providing a buffet for microorganisms and invertebrates—think of compost and decomposing cover crops as bird feeders for the tiny inhabitants of your dirt.

What *shouldn't* you do to your soil? While tilling can break some pest-bug cycles, the practice also demolishes populations of beneficial soil organisms like earthworms. Chemical fertilizers have a similar effect, as does leaving the earth bare of plants or mulch so that erosion and heat can remove nutrients from the soil.

Why not nurture an organic, no-till garden and let your soil workers do the job of tilling and fertilizing for you? (I explain how to begin and maintain a no-till garden in *The Ultimate Guide to Soil*.) Then you'll have a healthier garden, tastier vegetables . . . and won't have to work nearly as hard!

Invasive, but Beneficial

The average gardener doesn't realize that many of the invertebrates living in our soil and compost piles aren't native to the United States. All of the common woodlouse species in garden habitats (including pill bugs and sow bugs) were accidentally introduced from Europe, while the same is true of many of our earthworms and compost worms. As an environmentally-friendly gardener, should you be alarmed?

In most cases, the answer is no. However, it's worth taking a few steps to protect the native habitats around your garden. Invasive pill bugs don't seem to wander into the woods, but earthworms do,

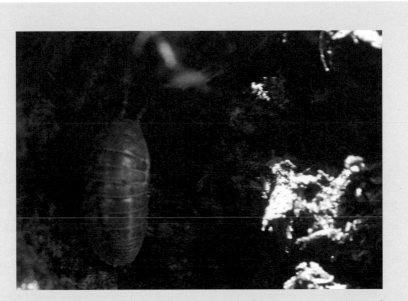

Pill bugs and sow bugs (also known as woodlice) are common residents of the compost pile. Most of the woodlice species found in the United States were introduced from Europe.

with devastating effects on forests far enough north that glaciation wiped out native earthworm species thousands of years ago. Since their introduction north of the glaciation line, invasive earthworms have changed soil dynamics by eating up the duff (leaf litter) on the forest floor, which in turn has affected the trees and wildflowers that grow in those northern forests.

Even in areas home to native earthworms, invasives tend to gain a foothold in disturbed and fragmented woodlands. Scientists are beginning to realize that invasive earthworms in the South may be linked to the spread of invasive plants like the extremely troublesome Japanese stiltgrass, and that invasive worms might also compete with our forest salamanders.

What can you do to prevent these forest woes from getting worse? If you fish, never dump excess bait worms in the wild, and if you own a vermicomposting operation, steer clear of the highly invasive *Lumbricus rubellus*, a worm which can be identified by the lack of stripes between segments and by the presence of a yellow underside. (The more common *Eisenia fetida*, with yellowish stripes between segments, isn't a native species either, but doesn't seem

(continued)

Native earthworms live primarily in the parts of the United States that weren't affected by the most recent glaciation. However, some worms have spread north into previously glaciated territory.

to cause problems in the wild.) If you live north of the glaciation line and near native woodland, you should also be very careful when moving soil around so that you don't introduce invasive earthworms into areas where they're now absent.

With those steps in place, even invasive woodlice and earthworms can be a boon to your garden. The former work hard to turn your compost pile while the latter do the same in your soil. As long as they stay out of the woods, these soil invasives remain on the list of good garden invertebrates, at least in my book.

Pollinators

Even beetles can be pollinators, as I discovered when I went out to check on the first spring flowers in the woods. In the garden, beetles are most likely to pollinate low-sugar flowers like those on pear trees, where the beetles also gnaw holes in the petals. As a result of the flower damage, beetles are considered "mess and soil pollinators," beneficial in the edible garden but unsightly among ornamentals.

Some insects you're probably already familiar with, like bumblebees, sweat bees (shown here), and carpenter bees, are high-quality pollinators.

While soil workers may be the most essential invertebrates in your garden, the flashiest good bugs are pollinators. Honeybees (*Apis* sp.) are the poster children for pollination since they produce delicious honey as well as moving pollen from flower to flower, but you can have a very well-pollinated garden without building an apiary. In fact, some scientists believe that an over-abundance of non-native honeybees causes declines in native-pollinator populations.

If you want to identify the insects visiting your flowers, I highly recommend the Xerces Society's beautifully-illustrated book titled *Attracting Native Pollinators*. However, you don't really need to figure out the species of each little insect on your apple blossoms in the spring. Nearly any bug on a flower is looking for pollen or nectar, and the pollen-hunter is likely to accidentally move pollen to the next flower in the process. Your goal should simply be to promote a diverse array of pollinators in the garden throughout the year.

Allowing clover and other weeds to grow in your lawn will keep the bees happy.

How will you know if your pollinator population *isn't* up to par? If you find cucumbers fat at one end and skinny at the other, baby summer squash that are rotting at the blossom end, blackberries with only a few plump lobes, or lopsided apples with a big side and a little side, your garden isn't seeing proper pollination. In some cases, inadequate pollination can be due to bad weather during bloom time, but if you notice problems, your first step should be to ensure that you're providing

Virgin's bower and other wild plants will feed pollinators like this honeybee if you allow the edges of your garden to run wild.

the proper habitat for wild pollen movers. (There's not much you can do about a cold spring.)

Attracting native pollinators can be nearly as simple as keeping your soil invertebrates happy. First, make sure you have wild or cultivated flowers blooming for as much of the year as possible, and remember that tiny bees may fly only 600 feet or less each day in search of food. The Xerces Society recommends big patches of flowers at least three feet in diameter so the clumps are easy for insects to see during their aerial commute, with smaller rows of flowers tempting the pollinators to continue their explorations out into your garden. The goal is to tempt a healthy population of pollinators into taking up residence on your homestead so they're raring to go when your fruit trees bloom in the spring and your cucumber flowers unfurl in the summer, needing their services.

- Encourage at least three different types of pollinator-friendly flowers in your garden each season.
- Plants marked with an asterisk are in the carrot, mint, or aster family and are particularly helpful for miniature pollinators.

Bloom Times of Pollinator-Attracting Plants

Spring:

- alder (pollen only)
- almond
- asparagus
- black locust
- blueberry
- borage
- cherry
- clover

- crocus
- dandelion*
- henbit*
- maple
- mustard
- peach
- plum
- poppy

- purple dead nettle*
- radish
- rose
- rosemary*
- serviceberry
- squill
- vetch
- willow

Summer:

- alfalfa
- basswood
- bee balm (and wild bergamot)*
- blackberry
- borage
- buckwheat
- clover
- coneflower*
- corn (pollen only)
- cosmos*
- fennel*
- fireweed
- globe thistle*
- hollyhock
- lavender*
- Mexican sunflower*
- milkweed
- mint*
- mustard
- oregano*
- partridge pea
- radish
- ragweed (pollen only)*
- raspberry
- rose
- Russian sage*
- sourwood
- stonecrop
- sumac
- sunflower*
- sweet marjoram*
- thyme*
- tulip-tree
- vetch
- viper's bugloss
- virgin's bower
- yarrow*

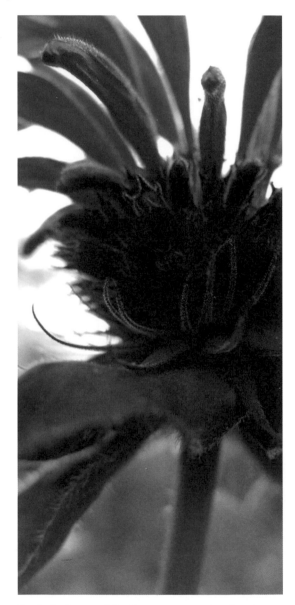

Bee balm is one of the flowers we use to attract pollinators to our garden.

Autumn:

- aster*
- boneset*
- cosmos*
- fireweed
- goldenrod*

- ironweed*
- Joe Pye weed*
- mountain mint*
- smartweed
- sneezeweed*

- stonecrop
- sunflower*
- wingstem*

These tables suggest some plants that are particularly good for attracting pollinators, focusing on species that you may already have growing in or around your garden. When choosing pollinator plants, remember that showy, cultivated flowers (like irises and modern roses) have often been bred to reduce their output of pollen and nectar. So wildflowers or old-fashioned cultivated plants (like single-petaled roses) are a better bet for your pollinator garden.

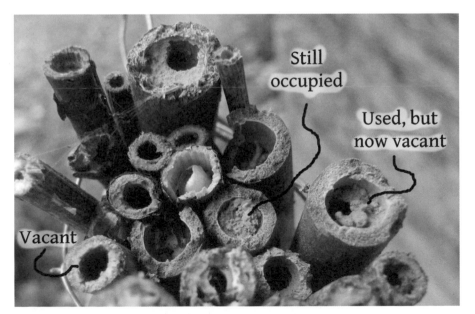

Some pollinators lay their eggs inside hollow stems, which the insects fill with food for their young before capping the ends with mud. You can make simple nest bundles for native bees by cutting bamboo of various diameters, making sure that one end is plugged by the node and that the other end is hollow. Hang your nest bundles horizontally under your eaves or in another dry spot, and the bees will lay eggs over the summer that will hatch in the spring.

In addition, members of the carrot, mint, and aster families, with their many tiny flowers in each head, are particularly useful if you'd like to attract the smallest pollinators. You should aim to have at least three different types of plants blooming in the spring, three in the summer, and three in the fall, and should be sure to cover the very early spring and late fall when pollinators are often in dire need of food.

Next, ensure that the wild pollinators have nesting sites available. Although you *can* build nest sites for pollinators, just letting the stems of plants like sunflowers and goldenrod stand

In addition to needing flowers for nectar and requiring specific host plants for their caterpillars to eat, butterflies are attracted to sources of salt. These gaudy pollinators often congregate at the edges of drying puddles, on damp manure, or where humans and other animals have peed.

through the winter will help out many species. Some pollinators need patches of bare soil, while yet others require a bit of nearby woodland. In general, letting the edges of your yard go wild will do much of the work of attracting native pollinators for you.

If you want to get a bit fancier, you can make a butterfly feeder . . . by peeing on the ground. Although nectar is a high-energy food source, the sweet liquid tends to lack salt, so butterflies and other nectar-eaters need to track down another source of this important nutrient. Male butterflies, in particular, spend a lot of time puddling—gathering around drying puddles or other sources of salt. Later, the males will pass a package of salt to the females as a gift when they mate.

The greater bee fly (*Bombylius major*) is a good pollinator, but the insect also parasitizes solitary bees and wasps.

Of course, as in the world of the soil, not all pollinators are purely allies of the garden. For example, the pollinator shown above is a fly that mimics a bee. Since the species appears so bee-like, the greater bee fly is able to get close to the burrows of solitary bees, into which it flings its eggs. When bee-fly eggs hatch out, the larval flies feed on larval bees, often killing the latter. However, as with most parts of garden ecology, bee flies still have an important niche in the ecosystem—there's no balance without predators as well as prey.

Gardening with Beneficials in Texas

By Eric Paulus

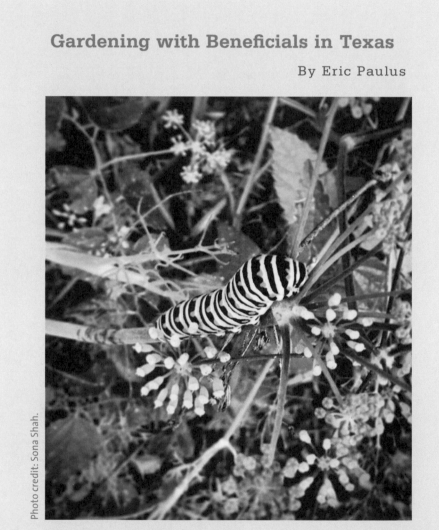

Photo credit: Sona Shah.

A black swallowtail caterpillar munches on dill.

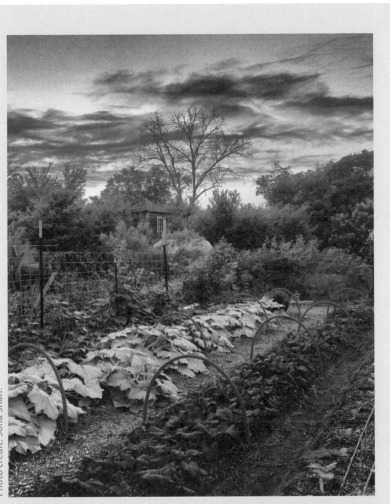

Avoiding all chemicals, even organic ones, has promoted a healthy garden ecosystem on Eric's farm.

Providing habitat for insects is my favorite part of gardening. At my current location, I'm a bit more than three years into creating an ecological balance. I garden commercially, but never use any "organic" sprays (no neem, Bt, etc.). I am absolutely seeing the benefits now. No major outbreaks as they are quickly mitigated.

My favorite helper plants include yarrow, tansy, parsley, khella (*Ammi visnaga*), and cilantro for the little wasps and hoverflies. We use a borage hedge as a green lacewing nursery. Radish flowers,

(continued)

Photo credit: Sona Shah.

Eric and his wife run a small urban farm in East Austin, Texas. To learn more, go to www.regenerationatx.tumblr.com.

African blue basil, tusli, chamomiles, cornflowers, and any allium flowers also attract all sorts of life in the garden.

And, surprisingly to me, the absolute best is fennel. Every day, all day, the flowers are covered with the most diverse number of species, including literally dozens of varieties of wasps at one time.

I know I'm forgetting many, but all these are great to include in the garden. It's also important to have various types of flowering plants throughout the year. For me, this means letting many naturally adapted plants (weeds) flower, especially in the winter.

Ladybugs are the classic garden predator. Brian Cooper attracts ladybugs early in the season by growing bachelor's buttons, and he finds that his efforts result in a healthy ladybug population for the rest of the year.

Predators

Speaking of predators, the third group of wholly-positive invertebrates is the bugs that consume bad insects. Spiders, centipedes, dragonflies, mantids (a.k.a. praying mantises), ambush bugs, assassin bugs, lacewings, ladybird beetles (a.k.a. ladybugs), ground beetles, true wasps, digger wasps, hoverflies, and robber flies all subsist primarily or entirely on other insects during some stage of their life cycle.

Although many of the species listed above are generalist predators, eating whatever ends up in front of them, all of these insects help keep pest population explosions in check. For example, I accidentally let the beetles on my green bean plants get

Praying mantises eat both good and bad insects. It's handy to know what mantis egg cases look like so you can leave the spongy structures behind when pruning fruit trees.

out of control one summer, and soon thereafter I saw a pair of praying mantises move in to take advantage of the bounty. Sure, the mantises might have been eating butterflies yesterday, but I consider them beneficial insects because they eat at least as many bad bugs as good.

Another category of predators is the parasitoids. Braconid wasps, ichneumonid wasps, chalcid wasps, and parasitic flies all lay their eggs on other insects, and unlike true parasites, the wasps and flies eventually kill their hosts. That's great news in the garden since many of the prey insects are bad bugs, like tomato hornworms or bean beetles, so the parasitoids keep the pests under control. As a side note, in case you're scared of the term "wasp," all of the parasitic wasps mentioned above are too small to sting human gardeners.

Many gardeners fall in love with the idea of predatory and parasitic insects and decide to buy some of these critters to seed their garden. However, I believe that you really need to encourage these species at the ecosystem level. I've heard of people opening a container of expensive insects, only to have them all

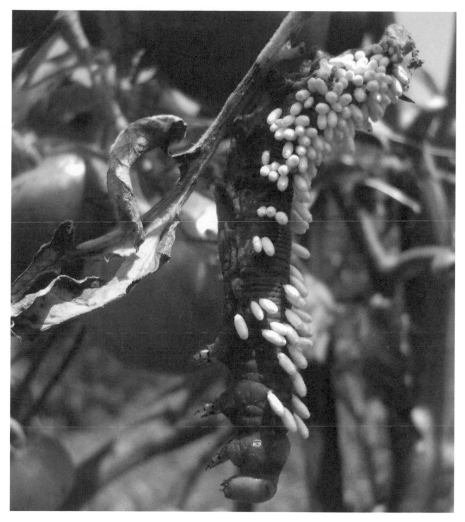

This hornworm is further along in the parasitization cycle than the one I pictured earlier. The caterpillar is dead in this photo and the wasps are getting ready to hatch out of their cocoons.

fly away because the garden isn't a hospitable environment for the predators to live in.

Instead of spending your money on insects, why not spend a bit of time encouraging the good bugs you already have to stick around and reproduce? Many predatory insects depend on flowers during some stage of their life cycle, so you can encourage them just like you did native pollinators by ensuring you have copious pollen and nectar sources available throughout the growing season.

In fact, you might receive double the benefit from any nest sites you put out for your native pollinators. Brian Cooper erected mason-bee blocks in his garden, and ended up encouraging mud daubers by providing wet mud nearby. Brian wrote: "When we went to harvest the bees, we found mud daubers also laid eggs in some of the unused cells. They collect food for their young inside the cell before they cap it with mud. I found one cell that was filled with caterpillars and a dauber larva, and another cell with a pupa of the mud dauber and just bug parts left over."

Pediobius foveolatus wasps parasitize Mexican bean beetle larvae, but you have to buy these tropical wasps each year to protect your bean planting.

All of these caterpillars were collected by a mud dauber (*Sceliphron* sp.), which paralyzed the plump morsels and stashed them in the nest chamber along with an egg. The dauber's baby will feast on the caterpillars as it grows.

Dragonflies (and toads) need a small pond in which to lay their eggs.

Assassin bugs, like this immature wheel bug (*Arilus cristatus*), use their long mouthparts to suck other insects dry.

Weedy edges will also encourage predatory insects since the predators need to be able to find lots of insects to eat even when your garden pests are under control. In addition, dragonflies need a pond into which they can lay their eggs, and many insects will benefit from having a very shallow body of water from which they can drink. In general, when attracting predatory insects, it's imperative not to use any pesticides (even organic ones) and to allow low levels of pest insects to fly under your radar. If there aren't any bad bugs around, your predatory insects won't have anything to eat and will go somewhere else.

In fact, you've probably sensed a theme throughout this chapter. To encourage the good bugs, let nature move into your garden. Leave things alone and the beneficials will come.

Attracting Predators with Weeds

By Roberta Walker

Roberta Walker shows off a day's harvest in September 2013.

Here in our corner of Northwest Missouri, we are fortunate enough to have a large population of Chinese mantids (*Tenodera aridifolia sinensis*). Come midsummer, I can hardly take a step through the garden without spotting one!

Also abundant in our area, however, is the very destructive and dreaded squash bug. I'm sure most readers of this book can relate to this nuisance in the garden. It is my belief that our population of mantids is the primary reason I am even able to harvest squashes and pumpkins, or even cucumbers and melons (since the squash bugs are non-discriminating).

I understand that mantids can also be somewhat relentless in their hunt for food, preying upon another generally popular "good bug," the ladybug. And so I take some extra measures to keep these two garden helpers apart.

(continued)

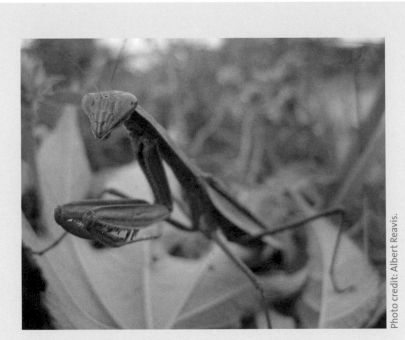

Photo credit: Albert Reavis.

Praying mantises keep squash bugs in check.

Because I am recruiting the mantids primarily to hunt down my squash bugs, I am sure to leave tall, woody-stemmed weeds (mostly giant ragweed) on the north side of my squash and cucurbit patches. Mantids enjoy skulking about these weeds in their off time, searching for mates and a place to establish oothecae (egg-sacks).

For the ladybugs, I plant dill and coriander along the edge of a hardy, wild patch of Queen Anne's lace. In my experience, these plants tend to attract ladybugs. It's also no coincidence that I choose to plant my peas near this "ladybug patch" to keep my aphid population in check.

I know for some this seems a disastrous approach to pest management. Leave such heavy-seeding weeds right next to the garden? Well, yes! Much like Anna (in fact, largely because of Anna), I enjoy the no-hassle method of drowning my weeds away with kill mulches. So whenever I feel as if these patches are beginning to intrude on garden territory, I simply break out the cardboard and violà! Not only do I put the weeds back in their place, but I add just a tad more fertility to my beds as well.

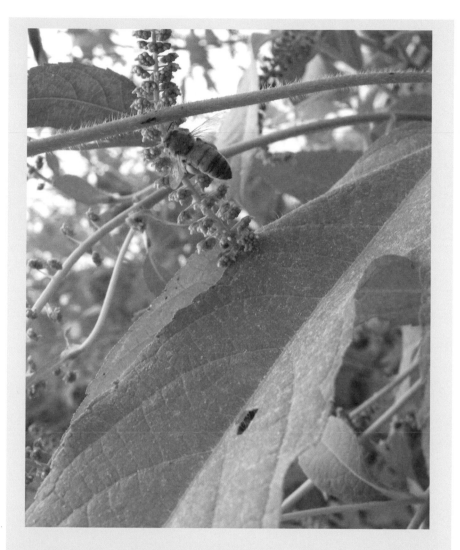

In addition to providing a mantis habitat, ragweed is also an excellent pollen source for honeybees and wild pollinators. However, allergy sufferers will prefer to cut the plants down before they bloom.

Chapter 12:
Helpers with Backbone

The previous chapter may have made it sound like good bugs are the holy grail of bad-bug control. However, it also helps to pay attention to the wider ecosystem when managing populations of pest insects. Even though you may not realize it, your bug problem might have actually started with a decision to eradicate snakes from your orchard or turtles from your tomato patch. So I'll spend a bit of time in this penultimate chapter answering the question: Which vertebrates are garden friends and foes?

Mammals

Deer are one of the few vertebrates with no redeeming value in the garden.

I'm going to skim over large mammals since most people are familiar with these creatures and will soon learn which ones are helpful or problematic in the garden. In both my Virginia and Ohio gardens, deer have been our worst large-mammal problem. But bloggers in South Africa report monkeys tearing apart their gardens, wild boars root up Japanese gardens, and parrots (instead of mammals) wing in to eat Australian gardens to the ground.

Among slightly-smaller American mammals, woodchucks (a.k.a. groundhogs) and rabbits are also problematic garden browsers, while skunks are mostly beneficial (although they can root up the garden inappropriately while trying to find their favorite foods: beetle grubs and cutworm larvae). One blog reader reported that turkeys peck open nearly ripe cantaloupes in search of seeds, and many have lost apples, pears, or corn to marauding raccoons. In general, I suspect most of us would prefer that all large mammals steer clear of our gardens.

Then there are the small mammals, which mostly consist of little critters that look like mice to the untrained eye. Small mammals can be good, bad, or neutral in the garden, so it's handy to know which animal is which.

Voles are mice-relatives that tunnel through the garden, gnawing on potatoes and carrots, eating the bark around the base of young fruit trees, and generally making trouble. You can tell voles from other small mammals by their rounded bodies, long fur, small ears, and short tails. We've found that a good dog and cat provide quality vole control

This shrew, caught by our dog, was once a beneficial part of the garden ecosystem.

in the garden, although you may have to put up with churned earth where your dog obsessively chased the vole back along its underground trail.

Shrews and moles are often blamed for the damage done by voles, but these species are insectivores and live almost entirely by eating both good critters (like earthworms) and bad critters (like slugs) in your soil. Shrews can be distinguished from voles by the fact that their ears are concealed by fur and their teeth are often stained brown. Moles are larger, with long-nailed, paddle-like front feet used for digging, and with eyes and ears concealed by fur. Mole tunnels are another giveaway that you're dealing with insectivores—in addition to the shallow runways that both voles and moles create, moles alone excavate deeper tunnels then mound the earth on the surface a bit like crayfish do. Unless you're trying to create a perfectly flat lawn, you should be happy when you see signs of shrews and moles since the insectivorous mammals prove that your soil ecosystem is in balance. You can encourage shrews and moles in the same way you encourage smaller soil workers—by feeding the soil with rich organic matter but otherwise leaving the earth alone.

The last type of small mammal you may notice in the garden is bats. These aerial predators eat large quantities of flying insects, so they can make their hunting grounds more habitable to humans. Bats don't have much impact on the garden itself, though, so I'll leave you to research more about these fascinating furry fliers on your own.

Birds

Like small mammals, birds can be either good or bad in the garden. Despite the occasional crows digging up sprouting corn kernels and cardinals eating the fruits from berry bushes, most birds we see in our garden seem to be acting as beneficial predators near the top of the garden food chain—in other words, they're

Phoebes are common predators of garden insects.

eating insects. *Edible Forest Gardens: Volume 2*, by Dave Jacke, lists the following birds as particularly beneficial in the garden for their insect-consumption skills: swifts, woodpeckers, flycatchers (including the phoebe, which is a common garden resident in the eastern U.S.), vireos, chickadees, titmice, nuthatches, brown creepers, wrens, bluebirds, wood warblers, tanagers, and orioles. As an added bonus, I've noticed that birds enjoy perching on stakes and trellises in the garden, depositing their manure around the bases of the plants below.

Woodpeckers deserve a special mention since they seem to be good friends of fruit trees. In *Organic Orcharding*, Gene Logsdon reports that promoting woodpeckers by leaving natural woodland adjacent to your orchard can reduce overwintering codling moth larvae by 52 percent, and one of our readers emailed me to say that woodpeckers in his yard were eating borers in his apple trees. Like several other types of birds, woodpeckers are cavity nesters, so

This downy woodpecker is pecking apart a praying-mantis egg case, but woodpeckers are also prone to eat borers and codling-moth larvae on fruit trees.

they can be encouraged with appropriate birdhouses, or by leaving standing-dead trees outside your garden perimeter.

Whole books exist on the topic of encouraging birds in your garden, but the gist usually boils down to providing them with nesting habitat, with protective cover (bushes, hedges, or brush piles), and with food. I'll just add two brief notes that are of particular interest for gardeners hoping to attract insect-eating birds to their yards. First, man-made houses are especially handy for cavity-nesters like bluebirds, since you can make the entrance hole just the right size to attract the species you're looking for. And, second, birdseed isn't the right feeding solution for many of the bug eaters—instead, you'll want to allow prey insects to live at low levels just like you did to promote predatory insects.

Reptiles

Lizards, like birds, are generally friends of the garden. Large lizards in other parts of the world (such as iguanas) may consume plants, but the little lizards most of us are familiar with prefer eating insects, spiders, centipedes, snails, other lizards, and young mice. Maybe they even eat baby voles? In any case, you can encourage lizards by providing small crevices in which the reptiles can hide. Rock piles and dry-stone walls are good shelters for lizards, and we've noticed that skinks (a type of lizard) particularly enjoy hiding out between logs in our woodshed.

Like most of their relatives, fence lizards are insect eaters.

Anoles are common garden-dwelling lizards in the southeastern United States.

People tend to be afraid of snakes, but many of these slender creatures are actually vital parts of the garden ecosystem, acting as predators of worms and other ground-dwelling invertebrates and (in some cases) loosening the soil as they burrow through the earth. My stance on snakes is very similar to my stance on

The eastern worm snake spends much of its time underground hunting earthworms. The snake also looks very much like a large worm when you dig it up.

garden insects—I know how to identify the poisonous snakes that live in my area, and then I assume that every other snake I see is good. Here in southwest Virginia, only rattlesnakes and copperheads have dangerous bites, and both are rare in the garden.

Worms make up 80 percent of an average garter snake's diet.

How do you encourage beneficial snakes like these? Blog reader Brian Cooper wrote in to say: "A couple years ago, I started lining my garden beds with logs from fallen tree branches (~6 inches in diameter) to allow for some moisture retention and to keep mulch in the beds while defining the paths. What I did not realize was that I was making a perfect home for earth snakes. This year, for the first time, I saw one while I was digging out our swale paths and accidentally disturbed one of these edge logs. These snakes are reported to eat arthropods and slugs, like to live underground, and can be found under logs." Other ways to encourage snakes include making rock or wood piles as you would for lizards, providing brushy cover as you would for birds, and leaving the ground alone as you would for soil workers.

While snakes and lizards are nearly all allies of the garden, I'd have to say that box turtles (the most common turtle found in gardens in the eastern U.S.) are neutral. Box turtles have a

Although they *will* take a bite out of your tomatoes, box turtles are generally friends of the garden since they love to eat snails and slugs.

Box turtles lay their eggs in loose soil, especially in the rotting wood of hugelkultur mounds. Once we started adding wood to our forest garden, baby box turtles turned up year after year.

tendency to visit tomato patches and take one bite out of each ripe fruit, which can drive some gardeners crazy. Carry the turtles away, and they'll slowly but surely walk back to your garden and continue eating those tomatoes, and then they'll head over to clean up the dropped berries beneath your raspberry plants. On the other hand, if you can handle a few nibbles on your fruits, box turtles will pay their way by consuming large quantities of problematic snails and slugs (as well as friendly earthworms), so I enjoy seeing these shelled reptiles in my garden. Box turtles move into the same kinds of environments that snakes and lizards enjoy, but turtles are particularly sensitive to chemical use.

Amphibians

Gardeners may have mixed feelings about reptiles, but amphibians are usually welcomed with open arms. And with reason—frogs and toads live entirely on invertebrates like insects, spiders, centipedes, millipedes, snails, and earthworms. To attract toads, many books recommend making houses out of upturned flowerpots with a door broken out of one side, but I've found that these warty amphibians prefer hanging out under the mulch in my vegetable garden instead. Toads became even more plentiful in my yard after I installed a small water garden, and the warty amphibians love spending time under a pallet my husband used as a temporary porch on swampy ground beside one miniature pond.

Toads hide under mulch during the day and come out at night or during rains to hunt garden slugs.

If you live outside North America, chances are you're unfamiliar with salamanders, and even many residents of the U.S. confuse these amphibians with lizards. Their scale-less, moist skin, though, is a dead giveaway that salamanders are relatives of frogs and toads, and that they depend on moisture of the surrounding environment to stay alive. If you maintain a heavy mulch in your garden, you may soon find mole salamanders (along with toads) moving in to eat your insects, worms, snails, and slugs.

Jackie Wilson emailed to tell me that, in her Pacific Northwest garden, "the slug problem was insane" until she started encouraging salamanders and toads with "little ponds in tall grasses, large damp compost piles with lots of coarse vegetable matter (like corn stalks and twigs), [and] rotting-log-lined berry beds . . . The little ponds I refer to are simply the biggest plant-pot saucers I can find, with a couple of flattish stones placed to make sure the critters can get in and out easily, next to an overturned container of some sort for snug cover. These are located in out-of-the-way

Mole salamanders spend most of their life in the earth.

wildish areas, which describes about ⅔ of the perimeter of my garden . . . Love those amphibians, and they are much lower maintenance than ducks."

Farm Animals

Speaking of ducks, if you mention insect control to ten permaculturalists, at least nine will tell you to invest in these aquatic poultry. Others sing the praises of chickens, guineas, and muscovies, while geese are recommended as weeders of your garden. The idea is to utilize stacking—a central permaculture tenet—to gain multiple yields from the same garden space, all while letting your livestock do some of the farming work for you.

Poultry *do* have a lot of potential in the garden, but you'll find that it requires more effort to incorporate livestock into your garden than to simply encourage wildlife to do the same job for you.

The trouble is that all poultry will eat (or mash down or scratch up) your garden plants if they're not managed carefully. That caveat aside, if you're going to raise poultry anyway, why not find a way to get them to eat some bad bugs in the garden too?

We've had the most first-hand experience with chickens, which we consider great friends for cleaning up weeds and soil insects on fallow ground. Chicken tractors are a handy way to keep your chickens in one small area so

We don't let our chickens run freely through the garden, but we do use the poultry to turn pest insects like Japanese beetles and cicadas into nutritious eggs.

they don't toss around mulch, demolish tomatoes, and scratch up seedlings throughout the garden, and you can also let chickens run free in a summer-only garden during the cold season when

A chicken tractor is a great way to utilize chickens in the garden without letting your vegetables suffer from the birds' destructive habits.

nothing is growing. Harvey Ussery suggests that bantams may be a slightly better choice than standard-size chickens when free ranging in active gardens since bantams don't scratch as much, but any chicken is going to be a problem in an active vegetable garden. In an orchard or other perennial planting, though, chickens may be just what you need for insect control, as long as you ensure the birds have enough space so that they don't over-fertilize your plants.

Unlike chickens, which can provide eggs and meat, guineas are usually just raised for meat (or for eye candy). In the garden, guinea fowl are handy since they're reputed to control squash bugs, ticks, grasshoppers, and snails. I haven't heard from anyone who free ranges guineas in their vegetable gardens, but I suspect there would be similar caveats to those mentioned about ducks below.

So that brings us to the permaculture poster-child—ducks. I'll admit up front that my personal experience with ducks lasted only one season, but many premier permaculturalists have shared their extensive wisdom on the topic. First of all, there's the potential—ducks adore slugs, insects, and worms, while Muscovies (a type of duck) are even known to hunt down flies. Meanwhile, the same ducks produce delicious and nutritious eggs and meat for their human keepers. However, as one of our blog readers reported, "[Ducks] are very destructive in the veg garden. We fence them out of the veg garden completely."

Carol Deppe, author of *The Resilient Gardener*, is perhaps the most-experienced duck-keeper in permaculture circles today. She loves ducks for their ability to control slugs in her Pacific Northwest garden, but she warns, "When it comes to greenery, ducks eat virtually everything people do, and more besides. So if you just turn a flock of ducks into a garden, you won't have a garden for long." Unlike chickens, ducks don't scratch, but their big feet do crush tender plants, their wet manure makes vegetables much less appealing, and their voracious appetite means they eat up everything in sight.

Ducks hunt through mulch with their bills rather than with their feet, so they tend to do less damage than chickens do. On the other hand, the waterfowl will eat most plants, so they can't be left in a vegetable garden unattended.

How does Deppe work around these duck foibles? She fences ducks into areas just beyond the garden, where their droppings attract slugs that are promptly snapped up by the poultry. Deppe raises Ancona ducks and reports that the fowl can be kept in by fences as low as two feet high, provided that the ducks have plenty of food and water and aren't separated from their friends.

Carol Deppe also lets ducks forage through her garden at intervals when she's standing by to keep an eye on them. She reports that ducks prefer insects and slugs over other food choices, so the birds will eat the pests first before chowing down on your tomatoes. However, you'll want to protect seedlings and low-growing greens before letting ducks into the garden for even these short field trips.

As appealing as it may be to imagine that poultry will take care of pest insects, the truth is that if you really care about your garden, all livestock will need to be fenced out of your vegetables most of the time. That's why I primarily focus on ecosystem-based pest-control techniques in this book. While you have to mind ducks as they hunt slugs in your garden, no one has ever complained about a the actions of a toad.

Scratching up Codling Moths

Dave Miller, who lives in Washington state near Portland, Oregon, uses wild birds and other critters to keep codling moths to a minimum. "I don't have any chickens or other permaculture animals—instead I try to use wild animals for those things," Dave explained.

In his area, codling moths are a "horrendous pest." Although putting a nylon stocking over each young fruit has achieved some success in the past, Dave notes that "those are a lot of work." This year, Dave's trying something new—a daily dose of sunflower seeds tossed around the base of each of his apple trees over the winter.

Dave Miller tosses sunflower seeds under his apple trees in the winter to tempt wildlife to scratch up codling-moth larvae.

"Here is my logic with that," Dave wrote. " Codling moths overwinter as larvae in bark crevices or in the leaf litter under the tree. I noticed that when I throw birdseed on the ground, the birds' natural instinct is to scratch the ground, even though the seed is sitting on top of the soil. When I throw birdseed under my apple trees, the birds happily scratch away for hours. I theorize that during the winter, if a bird uncovers a larva, the bird will gobble it up. Even if the birds don't eat the larvae, the insects will be exposed to the elements, which will probably make the insects unhappy and might even kill them."

In addition to the towhees and other birds that visit Dave's orchard feeding station, he notes that a second shift comes by at night, including squirrels, rabbits, raccoons, and opossums. The mammals and birds deposit manure at the same time they scratch up the ground, so their actions do double-duty to help the trees.

Will Dave's codling moth pressure be lower this year because of his bird-feeding campaign? The jury's still out, but I wanted to share this innovative technique with you anyway so you can experiment with the idea in your own garden. Maybe you can find a way to lure skunks to your lawn when Japanese beetle grubs are close to the surface, or perhaps you can bring gnatcatchers to your peaches

Nylon stockings act as a physical barrier, preventing codling moths and other problematic insects from laying their eggs in young fruits.

just as the Oriental fruit fly larvae emerge. Get creative and you could be talking wild animals into doing the garden pest-control work for you!

Afterword:
An Integrated Approach to
Pest Management

Dr. Arthur Trese runs the Ohio University Learning Garden using Integrated Pest Management techniques.

While the permaculture technique of building a bug-resistant ecosystem is inherently appealing, most gardeners will occasionally be forced to lower their standards if they hope to harvest an abundant crop. Scientists have a name for this process of aiming for the stars but accepting reality when necessary—integrated pest management (or IPM for short). In a nutshell, IPM involves understanding how pest insects fit into the ecosystem, using preventative measures like row covers and hand-picking when possible, then hitting population explosions with the lowest levels of effective insecticides when all else fails.

Dr. Arthur Trese of Ohio University's Learning Garden in Athens, Ohio, is a farmer well versed in IPM. He and a small cadre of enthusiastic interns run this 1.5-acre fruit and vegetable plot using vast quantities of elbow grease. Still, there are only so many hours in the day. So they have to work smart to harvest sufficient produce for twice-weekly sales to students, faculty, and members of the broader community.

To that end, Trese and his interns utilize a vast variety of pest-control methods, beginning with smart plantings meant to overcome invasions before they start. For example, summer squashes are set out successively throughout the season, with older plants quickly transitioning from productive members of the garden community into traps for squash vine borers. Insects lay their eggs on first-generation stems, those vines are removed, then younger plants are left pristine.

Wilted leaves—caused by a bacterial infection—are often the most visible sign that cucumber beetles have come to call.

Cucumber beetles are a bit trickier since this smaller pest hits the OU garden both hard and fast. To counteract the inevitable invasion, Trese begins with row covers when the plants are young, adding in the organic insecticide spinosad when pest populations start to soar. "We first used Bt in our garden," Trese notes. "But Bt only works on caterpillars. Spinosad is more broad-spectrum and is the only insecticide we currently use on our crops."

Trese has looked into chemical-free alternatives for the pesky cucumber beetles, mentioning pheromone traps that have recently come onto the market. "But traps are expensive," he notes as he pulls out a cucumber vine that succumbed to bacterial wilt borne by the small, yellow beetles. A pragmatist, he understands that

Spider flowers (*Cleome* sp.) are a favorite food for harlequin bugs. Having found that insecticidal oils don't faze this pest insect, Dr. Arthur Trese of Ohio University recommends hand squishing the insects attracted to spider flowers to lower pressure on nearby plants.

sometimes it's better to accept a certain level of losses than to spend more than you earn battling bugs.

Pragmatism doesn't prevent Trese from focusing on the eco-system, however. His garden is full of flowers that attract pol-linators and act as trap crops to condense problematic insects into one spot. Meanwhile, parasitic wasps are his slow-but-sure solution to cabbageworms on broccoli. "Wasp populations build naturally over the course of the season," Trese notes. "By fall, 80 percent of the caterpillars on broccoli are affected . . . but the cabbageworms keep eating anyway."

The caterpillars may eat, but the community does too. And after over a decade managing a garden that produces bags and barrels and bins of produce every week, Trese's integrated approach to pest control has clearly paid off. All it took was a few patches of flowers . . . and a lot of elbow grease.

Acknowledgments

This book wouldn't have reached your hands without the help of many people, each of whom deserves a huge thank-you. Readers of my blog always get top billing because their enthusiasm for homesteading topics (and willingness to share their experiences) is what keeps me writing. Specifically, Brian Cooper, Roberta Walker, Jackie Wilson, Dave Miller, Herrick Kimball, Leigh Tate, and Eric Paulus emailed me tips that ended up within these pages, and dozens of commenters on the blog helped me see the garden ecosystem from a broader perspective. I hope you'll join this vibrant community by visiting www.waldeneffect.org.

Additional assistance came from fellow gardeners who took time out of their busy schedule to allow me to visit their farms and pick their brains. Thank you, Art Trese and Kip and Becky Rondy for sharing your insect-control techniques when you would have rather been weeding.

Family and friends provided the next level of support for the book while it was a work-in-progress. My parents, Adrianne and Errol Hess, each read early drafts, then they both pushed my paperbacks on unsuspecting friends at farmer's markets, herbariums, and more. My husband, Mark Hamilton, took several of the photos that appear within these pages, and he also did the difficult job of helping me carve time out of our busy homesteading schedule to write. Moral support and other intangible aid came from a slew of people, including Wendy Jehanara Tremayne (author of *The Good Life Lab*), Rose Nell Hamilton and Jayne Wead (the best in-laws ever), Kayla Scarberry-Jacobs (my favorite fan and garden helper), and Frank Hoyt Taylor (movie-star neighbor extraordinaire). Closer to home, my two spoiled cats made the huge sacrifice of sharing my lap with a computer, during which time the felines were forced to seek my divided attention one cat at a time.

Last, but surely not least, thank *you* for reading! I hope *Bug-Free Organic Gardening* hit the spot and that your garden this year is a more vibrant, healthy ecosystem because of what you read within these pages. If you reach for your camera instead of for the Bt the next time a pest insect comes to call, then my journey to share natural pest-control techniques with you will have been a success.

Glossary

apiary: a collection of honeybee hives.

beneficial: good. In this book, I use the term to refer to animals that help maintain the overall health of your garden.

beer trap: a method of capturing slugs by setting a shallow dish of beer on the ground in the garden. Slugs crawl inside and drown overnight.

Bt: *Bacillus thuringiensis*. This soil-dwelling bacterium is often used as an organic pesticide. However, Bt kills a wide range of insects (which can include flies, mosquitoes, beetles, nematodes, and caterpillars of moths and butterflies), so the pesticide will harm some beneficials. In addition, Bt has been shown to have some small toxicity to humans and to the environment. Common trade names include DiPel and Thuricide.

borer: various types of insects that chew into the roots and trunks of trees or other plants.

caterpillar: a larval moth or butterfly.

cavity nester: an animal that lays its eggs and raises its young in holes in trees.

chemical fertilizer: fertilizers are added to the soil to provide nutrients for plants, the most notable of these nutrients being nitrogen, phosphorous, and potassium. Chemical fertilizers are man-made compounds in which the nutrients are supplied in their raw chemical form rather than bound to organic matter.

Carolina wrens are an example of cavity nesters, willing to lay their eggs in holes in trees, or in discarded flowerpots and unused mailboxes.

chicken tractor: a small pen for poultry that includes both the roosting area and an outdoor run. Chicken tractors are usually highly portable so they can be moved to a new spot every day.

codling moth: *Cydia pomonella*. An insect whose larvae feed on apples, pears, and English walnuts.

competition: among plants, competition usually involves individuals struggling to get more resources, such as light, nutrients, and water. Plants that are forced to compete with others may grow hardier, but seldom produce as much food from a human standpoint.

compost: decomposed organic matter that is often used to fertilize organic gardens.

cover crop: a plant grown to add fertility to a garden. For more information, see my ebook, *Homegrown Humus*.

crucifer: a member of the plant family Brassicaceae. Common garden crucifers include broccoli, Brussels sprouts, cabbage, cauliflower, collards, kale, mustard, radishes, and turnips.

CSA: short for community-supported agriculture, a CSA delivers a box full of varied produce to customers on a regular basis.

cucurbit: a member of the plant family Cucurbitaceae. Common garden cucurbits include cucumbers, gourds, melons, pumpkins, and squash.

cultivating soil: digging in the earth, usually with the purpose of controlling weeds or loosening hard ground. In the home garden, examples would include running a rototiller between rows to suppress weeds or using a hoe to kill weed seedlings. On a larger scale, cultivating can mean plowing before planting and churning up the soil between rows after planting.

decomposer: any organism that breaks down dead plants and animals into soil.

defoliate: to remove leaves. When involving insects, defoliation usually means that the animals are eating the leaves.

detergent: unlike soaps, detergents are synthetic cleaning products that use surfactants for superior cleaning in the kitchen and laundry room. Unfortunately, detergents are more harmful to plants than soaps are, so they have no place in the garden.

determinate tomato: a variety in which the fruits all ripen close to the same time.

diatomaceous earth: a crumbly soil made from fossilized diatoms that once lived in rivers, lakes, and oceans. Diatomaceous earth is often used as an organic pesticide because the substance irritates insects' exoskeletons and absorbs important oils, causing the insects to dry out and die. Diatomaceous earth only affects insects when the compound is dry, so use of the pesticide is not a problem for the environment. However, diatomaceous earth can irritate the skin, lungs, and eyes of people, and the dry compound is a broad-spectrum insecticide that will kill most invertebrates in its path.

disperse seeds: moving seeds from one spot to another. Many plants count on animals to disperse their seeds.

ecosystem: a community of interacting plants and animals.

egg case: the structure that surrounds and protects eggs.

fallow: part of a garden that is not being used to grow food at the current time.

fertilization: adding nutrients to the soil, often in the form of compost, manure, chemical fertilizers, compost tea, or urine.

generalist predator: an organism that will eat many kinds of animals rather than just one type.

grub: a larval beetle.

hardy plant: a plant that is able to survive cold or other difficult conditions.

herbivore: an animal that eats plants.

A wolf spider is an example of a generalist predator since the spider will eat any small insect it can catch.

high tunnel: also known as a hoop house, high tunnels are unheated greenhouses created by stretching plastic sheets over a simple frame.

hugelkultur: a method of adding rotting wood to a garden to increase the organic matter content of the soil. The wood is usually buried in ground.

insecticidal soap: a special kind of soap sprayed on plants to kill insects. Insecticidal soaps work by disrupting the insects' cell membranes. Although considered organic, insecticidal soaps are broad-spectrum insecticides that kill most soft-bodied insects upon contact.

invertebrate: animals without a backbone.

iron-phosphate bait: a type of purchased poison used to kill slugs and snails. Trade names include Sluggo and Escar-Go.

larva: an active, immature form of an insect, such as a caterpillar or a grub.

leafy greens: vegetables in which the leaves are eaten. Common examples of leafy greens include kale, mustard, Swiss chard, and collards.

micronutrient: a mineral that plants require but only use in very small amounts. The eight main micronutrients are boron, chlorine, cobalt, copper, iron, manganese, molybdenum, and zinc.

monoculture: a large planting of a single crop. For example, a five-acre cornfield.

mulch: a substance (usually plant matter) laid on the surface of garden soil to hold in moisture, prevent weed germination, and increase organic matter content of the earth.

mycorrhizal fungi: beneficial fungi that team up with plant roots, capturing minerals from deep in the soil and trading those nutrients for sugars provided by plants.

neem oil: oil pressed from the fruit and seeds of an evergreen tree, *Azadirachta indica*. Neem oil is used as an organic pesticide, but the oil is a broad-spectrum chemical that will kill most insects that the substance comes in contact with.

nematode: a very small kind of worm. Some nematodes harm plant roots.

nest site: a spot where an animal lays its eggs.

no-till: a method of gardening that strives not to disturb the soil. Commercial-scale no-till farmers often use toxic herbicides to kill weeds in lieu of plowing, but no-till gardeners simply lay down heavy mulches and hand-weed.

nutrients: minerals and other substances that plants and animals need.

organic matter: dead plants and animals and their waste products, which are applied to soil as fertilizers or mulches. Garden examples include manure, compost, leaves, and straw. The dark-colored humus found in soil is also referred to as organic matter.

permaculture: sustainable farming systems. Because the term "organic" has become industrialized in recent decades, gardeners who are more serious about growing food in harmony with the earth replaced the term "organic" with the term "permaculture."

pesticide: a chemical that kills insects.

pheromone: a chemical emitted by an animal to communicate with other animals.

Butterflies bring beauty to the garden but are inefficient pollinators compared to wild and cultivated bees.

pollination: fertilizing a potential fruit by transferring pollen from one flower to another or by transferring pollen from one part of a flower to another part of that flower.

predator: an animal that eats other animals.

pupa: the intermediate form between a larva and an adult insect. Pupae are often protected inside cocoons.

pyrethrin: an organic pesticide derived from *Chrysanthemum cinerariiaefolium*. Pyrethrin—and the related, artificially created pyrethroids—are often used to eradicate cabbage loopers, cucumber beetles, leafhoppers, stink bugs, and thrips. However, bees are also very sensitive to pyrethrin, so the chemical may have negative effects on pollinator populations.

organic gardening: growing plants using only natural inputs. The definition of "natural" varies greatly, and some amendments that are allowed by current organic standards can be harmful to the environment.

pyrethrin: any of several types of chemicals derived from the plant *Chrysanthemum cinerariifolium*, extracts of which have been used as insecticides for approximately three thousand years. Pyrethrins impact insects much more severely than they do mammals, so the pesticide is considered moderately safe from a human point of view. However, there have been some cases of human illnesses caused by the chemical, fish are particularly sensitive to pyrethrin runoff, and honeybees are strongly affected by pyrethrin use in their habitat.

rhizobial bacteria: microorganisms that live within the root nodules of legumes. Rhizobial bacteria take nitrogen out of the air, converting the nutrient into a form that plants can use.

rock dust: finely crushed stones used to supply minerals to garden soil.

rotation: growing different types of vegetables in different parts of the garden each year. See *The Weekend Homesteader* for more information. Garden rotation can lower pest and disease levels.

row cover: a thin fabric laid over garden plants that lets air, light, and water through. Row covers keep pests out and can help protect plants from frost.

soap: a cleaning produce that has been in use for thousands of years. The natural ingredients used to create soaps make them safer in the garden than detergents are.

solitary bees: bees that don't live in colonies. Examples include mason bees, sweat bees, and carpenter bees. Honeybees are *not* a solitary bee since many individuals work together in one hive.

spinosad: an insecticide based on the bacterium *Saccharopolyspora spinosa*. Spinosad is a broad-spectrum insecticide that will kill most insects on contact.

sticky trap: a method of capturing pest insects after attracting them to a certain color or odor. Sticky traps kill insects by gluing the invertebrates to the surface of the sticky trap, similar to the way flypaper works.

stubble: the roots and lower stems left behind in a field when a crop is mown down.

till: to churn up the earth, usually with a plow or rototiller.

topdress: to add compost to the surface of soil, usually as a fertilizer.

weedy edge: part of the garden left alone to revert to wild plants.

Index

fungus gnats, 64

maple, 83

marigolds, 38

marsh slug, 17

melons, 37

Mexican bean beetle, 5, 21–22

Mexican sunflower, 84

midges, 10

midget milky garden slug, 17

milkweed, 84

milky garden slug, 17

Miller, Dave, 53, 114–116

miner bees, 77

mint, 84, 85, 86

minute pirate bugs, 10

mites, 4, 5

mole salamanders, 109, 110

mollusks, 4, 5

monkeys, 101

monoculture, 39

moths, 4, 5, 114–116

mountain mint, 85

mud daubers, 94, 95

mushrooms, 70

mustard, 83, 84

myriapods, 4, 5

N

Nardi, James B, 78

neem oil, 13, 19

nematodes, 38

nitrogen, 10, 41

nuthatches, 104

nutrition, plant, 40–42

O

oregano, 84

Organic Orcharding (Logsdon), 104

orioles, 104

P

paper wasps, 11

parasitoids, 92

parrots, 101

parsley, 89

partridge pea, 84

Paulus, Eric, 88–90

peach, 83

pee, 87

pepper maggot flies, 56

pesticides, 66–68, 96

pheromones, 15, 119

pheromone traps, 64

phoebe, 103, 104

physical barriers, 43–50

pill bugs, 78, 79

pirate bugs, 10

plant defenses, 28–29

plant nutrition, 40–42

Pleasant, Barbara, 47

plum, 83

pollination, 46

pollinators, 81–91

poppy, 83

potted plants, 43–45

poultry, 110–111

predators, 91–99

pumpkins, 37

purple dead nettle, 83
pyrethrins, 68

Q
Queen Anne's lace, 98

R
radish, 83, 84, 89–90
ragweed, 84, 99
raspberry, 84
rattlesnakes, 106
redworm, 76
reptiles, 105–108
resistance, of plants, to insects, 35–37
robber fies, 91
robins, 15
Rondy, Kip, 47
root maggots, 46
rose, 83, 84
rosemary, 83
rotenone, 68
row covers, 11, 13, 45–50, 118–119
Russian sage, 84

S
sage, 84
salamanders, 109, 110
salt, 86
saltwater, 70
serviceberry, 83
shrew, 101, 102
skinks, 105

slug, 8, 16–18, 56, 65–66, 70, 109
smartweed, 85
snakes, 106–107
sneezeweed, 85
soap and water, 61–63
soil workers, 75–80
soldier beetle, 74
sourwood, 84
spiders, 4, 5, 75, 91
spinosad, 11, 67–68
spotted cucumber beetle, 13
squash bug, 8, 18–19, 37, 46
squash vine borer, 8, 19–20, 30–32, 37, 46, 56, 67
squill, 83
sticky traps, 13, 15, 64–65
stink bugs, 27–28, 56, 68
stonecrop, 84, 85
striped cucumber beetle, 13
succession planting, 32
sumac, 84
sunflower, 84, 85, 86–87
sweat bees, 77, 81
sweet marjoram, 84
swifts, 104

T
tanagers, 104
tansy, 89
Tate, Leigh, 59
tawny garden slug, 17
thrips, 68
thyme, 84

About the Author

Anna Hess dreamed about moving back to the land ever since her parents dragged her off their family farm at the age of eight. She worked as a field biologist and nonprofit organizer before acquiring fifty-eight acres and a husband, then quit her job to homestead full time. She admits that real farm life involves a lot more hard work than her childhood memories entailed, but the reality is much more fulfilling and she loves pigging out on sun-warmed strawberries and experimenting with no-till gardening, mushroom propagation, and chicken pasturing.

She also enjoys writing about her adventures, both on her blog at www.waldeneffect.org and in her books. Her first paperback, *The Weekend Homesteader*, helped thousands of homesteaders-to-be find ways to fit their dreams into the hours leftover from a full-time job. In addition, her heaping handful of ebooks serve a similar purpose.